UNIQUELY HUMAN

Center Point
Large Print

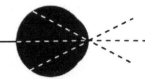

**This Large Print Book carries the
Seal of Approval of N.A.V.H.**

UNIQUELY HUMAN

Glimpses of Life

George Hillier

CENTER POINT LARGE PRINT
THORNDIKE, MAINE

This Center Point Large Print edition
is published in the year 2017 by arrangement with
the author.

The text of this Large Print edition is unabridged.
In other aspects, this book may vary
from the original edition.
Printed in the United States of America
on permanent paper.
Set in 16-point Times New Roman type.

ISBN: 978-1-68324-573-5

Library of Congress Cataloging-in-Publication Data

Names: Hillier, George, author.
Title: Uniquely human : glimpses of life / George Hillier.
Description: Large print edition. | Thorndike, Maine :
    Center Point Large Print, 2017.
Identifiers: LCCN 2017039266 | ISBN 9781683245735
    (hardcover : alk. paper)
Subjects: LCSH: Hillier, George—Literary collections. |
    Authors, Canadian—20th century—Biography. | Runners (Sports)—
    Canada—Biography. | Teachers—Canada—Biography. |
    Large type books.
Classification: LCC PR9199.3.H484 A6 2017 |
    DDC 818/.5409 [B]—dc23
LC record available at https://lccn.loc.gov/2017039266

Dedicated to my wife, Janemarie, with the feeling deep down in my heart how little I would have understood much about love, and how inconsequential my life would have been without her.

TABLE OF CONTENTS

INTRODUCTION

In recent years I have been busy putting this book together. As a result, I have recaptured the metaphorical images of growing up in St. John's, Newfoundland, Canada and immigrating to the United States as a young adult. Now I am eighty-one years old, and still continue to write in various venues including my website, Facebook, and as a blogger. I've enjoyed teaching English and Reading for over fifty years.

My background includes coming to America on a leadership scholarship to Boston University, earning both B.S. and Ed. M. degrees, along with completing advanced graduate study at Tufts University, earning certification in learning disabilities. Throughout my career I have taught at a variety of locations in Massachusetts including (Buckingham) Browne, and Nichols private school in Cambridge, at Pollard Junior High School in Needham, at Winchester High School, and Minuteman Technical Vocational High School in Lexington. I taught reading in the evening division at Northeastern University, and established a private reading clinic (K-12 and adult level) in my hometown of Arlington, Massachusetts. More recently, in 2000, I founded a learning center at St. John's Northwestern

Military Academy in Delafield, Wisconsin, where I continue to tutor as a volunteer.

As a young man I also developed an avid interest in running that consumed a great part of my time. My maximum effort led to success as a runner by holding Newfoundland's records for the one, three, six, and fifteen mile run and the marathon. I was inducted into the Newfoundland and Labrador Sports Hall of Fame in 1982 and 2009.

I've had my share of serious health issues including colon cancer, an aortic aneurysm, and two heart attacks. I am a survivor! The exciting thing is that I'm alive, still continue to write, and maintain a strong program of health and physical fitness.

Throughout the years, I have enjoyed the support of Janemarie, my wife of fifty plus years (seems like an eternity!), my two grown sons, George and David, and four grandchildren, Matthew, Caitlyn, Emily, and Jennifer. I hope you will enjoy reading and sharing my life's experiences.

ACKNOWLEDGMENTS

Janemarie kept telling me to continue writing as often as possible with the intent of writing a book. Also, she contributed its title *Uniquely Human*, since she felt that the title is a true reflection of my personality and character incorporated in my short stories.

I extend my full appreciation to the library staff in the Wisconsin towns of Delafield, Hartland, Oconomowoc, Pewaukee, and Waukesha. They provided me with their friendly cooperation and professional service by finding the research to support my needs.

Indeed, I would never have finished my work if I didn't have the support and guidance of Sharon Gruell who helped with the manuscript preparation and editing. She kept me on track by organizing my material before making my submission to the publisher.

Putting together material for a book can be most tiring except for those teachers, staff personnel, and friends who made everything possible with their inspiration, typing, and organizational skills: Lynette Ahlgren, Michelle Eigenberger, Doug Holmes, Luke Knoedler, Peg Koller, Stacy Menting, and John Thornburg. A special thank you is extended to Amy Karsten for her help with the front cover design. All their efforts and generosity of spirit are greatly appreciated. Rebecca Bogdanovich was very involved in reading my stories and providing suggestions that were invaluable to me.

Also, I owe a debt of gratitude to Jaime Buege, Director of Public Affairs and Communications at St. John's Northwestern Military Academy. She took my photograph and was successful in making an old man look his best.

The following articles were previously published in *The Evening Telegram*, St. John's Newfoundland: "A New Pair of Sneakers," January 28, 1998; "The Day I Raced the Streetcar," January 28, 1998; "Waiting for You in County Clare," March 6, 1998; "Even For a Fatalist, Life Goes On," August 26, 1998, and "A Tough Competitor and a Good Man," September 24, 1998. "From the Depths of a Nightmare Come Hope and Life" was previously published in the *St. Petersburg Times*, Clearwater, Florida, February 21, 1996.

I would like to thank all my doctors and the medical personnel who helped me to live long enough to write this book.

Janemarie and I are forever indebted to our long time friends, Ron and Charlene Kurth, who have been a source of never-ending support.

Ted and Maxine Pitcher, who share our

common roots in Newfoundland, can fully understand and appreciate our life's experiences.

Last but not least, I must thank Summer Ramsamy, the publishing consultant, and Sabrina Ali, the author account manager, at Friesen Press in Victoria, British Columbia. They worked with me patiently and directed me to fulfill all my obligations toward finishing my book.

LATE BLOOMER

I was invited to speak in chapel at St. John's Northwestern Military Academy in Delafield, Wisconsin on November 19, 2009. I spoke for 15 minutes and only used material that was pertinent. Around 300 cadets were present for my address to motivate them on their epiphany. Here is what I said:

I submit to you I had so much trouble learning how to read in my elementary years at Centenary Hall in St. John's, Newfoundland, Canada. For sure I was considered a late bloomer, or as I learned in time, I was born later than expected since I got caught up in the umbilical cord, unbeknownst to me. I guess I was never good with knots, anyway. Nevertheless, I learned that I had to work harder in school in order to keep up with the boys and girls in my class.

In spite of it all, my attitude towards learning was excellent and, undoubtedly, I put forth the finest effort, interest, and determination to succeed. I adored my teachers, especially the female ones, and loved the beautiful old school on Gilbert Street. I guess you'd agree, you teachers out there, I was hyperactive and full of energy and would get into many fights, if not every day, then every other day.

My sisters would usually say to my mother, "George got into another fight today!" I have no reason why I fought so much, yet, being so small in stature, I dare say I was most eager to prove myself to others and the world. I was always ready to box by accepting any contenders in school or out on the street.

My five sisters were quite bright, my older brother was very smart, and I was the one crying in the wilderness for all the help I could receive from my teachers and my mother in order to make some sort of progress. Years later I wrote my nostalgic feelings about those years at Centenary Hall:

O! Dick and Jane you had to read
with consciousness and never speed.
Miss Matthews' way would captivate
by teaching love, dispelling hate.
You bowed your heads and said a prayer
when your GOD'S GHOST was
    HEAVEN there.
Just when you'd cough or sneeze or sniff,
your sleeve became your handkerchief.
Your nose was cold, but it would show
your lips would catch the overflow.
And when THE SUN had lost its face,
COD LIVER OIL would take its place.
They say the war was settling in,
but trust was pride: you hoped we'd win.

Taffy apples at Mercer's Store
and banner car'mels by the score.
Hopscotch and marbles were a treat.
O, GIANT STEPS ON GILBERT STREET!
You could not let your mind contend
those precious years would have to end.

The effective use of mnemonic devices inspired me since I could memorize the acrostics and apply my facts to improve my learning dramatically. I would make up a nonsense word, for example, NAPAVAPCI, and turn it into a poem readily:

NOUNS are just the names of things like "snow" and "rice," "birds" and "rings."

ARTICLES are words "the" and "an": they point out nouns, "the" boy, "a" man.

PRONOUNS tell about nouns like "you" for woman, and "me" for clown.

ADJECTIVES describe nouns: "quacking" ducks and "pretty" gowns.

VERBS show action like "stir" or state like "is," or "was," or "were."

ADVERBS: They tell us then about such words as "how" or "why" or "where" or "when."

PREPOSITIONS precede a noun: "by," "for," "to," "at" or "in" the town.

CONJUNCTIONS: "and," "or," and "but" join words and clauses used instead of pauses.

INTERJECTIONS: Strong feeling words are "Ouch!" and "Oh!" "Bah!" and "Lo!"

It took ages for me to grasp the fundamentals of phonics and the rules and exceptions in spelling. I didn't spell or read satisfactorily until I was in the fourth grade. I seemed so stunned, for it was as if I could never even tell the difference between A BUMBLE BEE AND A BULL'S FOOT. Good grief!

I took Latin in high school and even advanced to taking it in college for two years. One Latin slogan gave me sound advice about enhancing my reading efficiency: "REPETITIO EST MATER STUDIORUM" that stands for "REPETITION IS THE MOTHER OF LEARNING." So it wouldn't be unusual for me to read a passage two, three, four, or even more times, to reinforce my knowledge and understanding.

I loved my teacher, Miss Matthews, and when I was told I was going to repeat the second grade, instead of being in despair, I was so excited since I adored her so much I never wanted to leave her anyway. O happy day! I am not so certain, though, if her heart was really set on putting up with the likes of me for two years in a row. O, my!

My mother would tutor me in the evening after tea and I dreaded it in the beginning. But she knew how far I was behind my schoolmates and realized there was no other alternative. Under her tutoring, I began to excel by reading more smoothly, making fewer mispronunciations, fewer omissions of words, fewer substitutions of words, and ended up with far less repetitions of words and phrases.

My Mom always made sure I was clean and tidy and would use the word "SCRUPULOUSLY" in her ministrations. Her suggestion came to me in this manner, "Make sure you wash your hands scrupulously clean!" Then I got the idea she meant REALLY clean. One of my mother's many loving gifts to our family was when she bought us the complete set of 20 volumes of THE BOOK OF KNOWLEDGE BY THE GROLIER SOCIETY. That was the time when she expanded our horizons of learning about the world and everything in it.

In grade six I was preparing for a test in Geography and read, studied, and reviewed my chapters well; I also wrote down in my scribbler important facts vital for improving my performance in this subject. Then she would quiz me over and over on the material to build up my confidence.

The next day I came home from school and was disgusted and told my mother I received only 67% on my test. She looked at me and, for sure, she knew the state of mind I was in at the time, "Don't worry, son! Into each life some rain must fall." I was relieved somewhat, but I also had a stubborn streak in me and spoke to her matter-of-factly, "Mom, if you and Dad were smarter, I dare say I would have gotten a much better grade." She never liked my remark and countered with this response, "O, no! You are just like your father's people!"

Gradually, I improved significantly by coming home in the afternoons, delivered my *Evening Telegram*s in the neighborhood, returned to my house, spoke to my mother, ate a slice of my mother's homemade bread with molasses and butter, and then took off to my bedroom to study my head off. I improved my grades so well that I came first in both grades seven and eight. My mother was so happy and congratulated me for doing such a good job. On the other hand, it was her tutoring during those years that made all the difference.

When she spoke, she was so happy for my hard work and success, "Now all you have to do is to follow through and come first in grade nine."

I told my mother in no uncertain terms, "Thanks Mom, but I won't be coming first anymore."

"Why not, son?"

"MOM, I MUST TELL YOU IT'S MUCH

TOO HARD! What I really want to do is to get out and play with my friends for a change."

I persisted and kept improving my grades at Curtis Academy and was awarded two scholarships for being on the honor roll and for improving on my conduct in my senior year. Above my photo in our yearbook is this caption: "HOW DANGEROUS IT IS THAT THIS MAN RUNS LOOSE!" Ye gawds!

My passion, though, was always about RUNNING. I got into dating when I was 14, but I was far too shy to call a girl out, for my heart would beat much faster than if I were out on the road running in a race. In other words, it was far easier to run four or five miles on a track and blow off steam than it was to ask a girl out to a movie matinee.

I'm not sure but my first year in college was a total disappointment. I thought I had everything together, and suddenly I was doomed to succeed in failure. I guess I received a big shock that was a dreadful escape from reality. Indeed, I honestly believe that my sister's death on April 21,1951, dealt me a heavy blow, when she was killed by a drunken driver in such a ghastly manner on Richmond Hill in Toronto, Ontario, Canada. I imagined all hell broke loose, yet there's no way I could blame her death as being an excuse for my having done so poorly in college. To say the least, the shock from it all was suddenly overwhelming.

I really didn't know what grief was till this tragedy happened to our family. I believe, out of guilt or fear, I must somehow bear as much as I can the cringing pain and sorrow of my sister's death. For sure, I will never forget my sister, and through the years she appears to me in a dream once in awhile that gives me some sense of stability in my life. So I have to accept everything lovingly now in order to return to the mainstream.

I went through the paces at Memorial College in St. John's, Newfoundland and as I would subtly put it, majored in RUNNING with a minor in PING PONG. I had my own taste of failure, and I didn't relish it one iota. Finally, I dropped out of college and went to work with the hope of returning when my life got better.

In 1955 I was awarded a full scholarship at Boston University and received my bachelor's degree in 1958. In the winter of 1955, I met Janemarie who was a student at Radcliffe College. I married her on December 19, 1956, and still kept up my running where I left off. I distinguished myself at B.U. in both track and cross-country, becoming captain of both in my senior year.

I believe that Janemarie straightened my life out soon enough by telling me, "I'm not interested in marrying a dumb jock. So you see where I stand now. I know you can do much better in academics and still keep up your running." I took what she said in earnest and accepted her ultimatum. What else was there to do? It didn't take me long to adjust, for I believe that running and marriage have much in common: all I had to do was to learn how to TOE THE LINE. Hmm.

In fact, I became more responsible and studied more diligently; consequently, I got A's in most of my courses and was awarded a Master's Degree in Education (Ed.M.).

At the same time, I excelled in my running in Canada and held the records in Newfoundland for the one mile, the three, six, and fifteen mile races, and the 26.2 mile marathon in 1952. Also, I broke the Canadian Marathon Record in 1956. Without being overly pretentious, on July 16 of 2009, I was inducted into the Newfoundland and Labrador Hall of Fame for all my running exploits in the 1950's.

I understand you cadets out there since I know you are expected to perform well in your academics, athletics, and military leadership. So you can see what I'm made of, but what does my story mean to you this morning? Well, let me tell you, "Set your goals high and maintain an excellent attitude towards your teachers and in all the courses you take."

I recognize so much personal and academic potential in you at the academy and wish you the greatest success in your future years. Do all you can to develop that burning desire within you to achieve your highest goals. Remember this, "You get what you work for, so you can count on it. ABOVE ALL, JUST GIVE IT EVERYTHING IT TAKES BECAUSE THAT'S WHAT IT TAKES TO GIVE."

Throughout my teaching career, I was in love with teaching in such a variety of systems in New England and elsewhere: private school at Browne & Nichols (now BB&N) in Cambridge, MA; public education at the elementary and secondary level, especially teaching reading at Pollard Junior High in Needham, MA and Winchester High School in MA; our own private school, Arlington Reading Clinic, for 36 years that covered kindergarten to the adult level; Minuteman Vocational Technical High School in Lexington, MA; teaching fellow at Tufts University Summer Institute; Northeastern University, Boston, by teaching reading in the evening division; and lastly, establishing in 2000 a Learning Center (now the Totzke Learning Center) in Delafield, Wisconsin, at St. John's Northwestern Military Academy.

Summarily, I must say you will pass through these halls but once; any good you can do for others, for your parents, for your teachers, for your academy, and for yourselves, do it now. Don't put off your goals for you will never pass this way again.

I would like to finish my address this morning with a poem by Hamlin Garland, a Mid-Westerner from these parts. I memorized this poem when I was in grade six in Newfoundland. It is one of my favorite pieces since it motivated me to face all kinds of challenges in life. I believe that it will also cheer you on with its deep sense of purpose:

DO YOU FEAR THE FORCE OF THE WIND?

Do you fear the force of the wind,
The slash of the rain?
Go face them and fight them,
 be savage again.
Go hungry and cold like the wolf.
Go wade like the crane.
The palms of your hands will thicken.
The skin of your cheek will tan.
You'll grow ragged and weary and swarthy,
But you'll walk like a man!

Good morning and God bless you all.

CURTIS ACADEMY MEMORIES

You walk up a rocky lane from Hamilton Avenue to your school, Curtis Academy, which burned down many years ago. You stand among the rubble and the ruin. Ghosts seem to stalk you. Yet for all that, you behold a sense of haunting beauty, as the green grass still grows begrudgingly among the masses of concrete, of how much your school used to represent.

Everything around the old place shakes your foundation. You even pick up a piece of concrete as a souvenir of your alma mater. The pause you make is curiously disturbing. Isn't it from a sort of futility, when the scene, the wasteland lying before you, has dissolved into nothingness? You look back over the years in reckoning history, more years than you wish to remember, and you begin to agree that you don't miss the school at all; instead, you miss the family.

When our principal, Mr. Fred Rowe, said goodbye in 1948, he left his message with us for all time:

"I shall take away many memories that will be with me as long as I live. But the best memory will not be the building itself, nor the classrooms, not the things we did. It will be the memory of you, boys and girls—the little ones in kindergarten struggling bravely to enter a new world; the young men and women in the upper grades, approaching the time when they must set out on another great adventure; the sea of bright, eager faces that faced me at every assembly, your vitality and kindness, your readiness to do the right thing, your determination never to let the school down. All these memories of you will stay with me."

Among the debris, you still hear the strains of your old school song:

Hurrah! Hurrah! Curtis Academy,
Thy sons and daughters, we
Do proudly sing
And loyal hearts we bring
To Curtis Academy

Though Curtis never got to rise up to the level of a college like St. Bon's, Prince of Wales, Bishop Field or Bishop Spencer, we were rightly named an academy because we had our commander-in-chief, since we were his onward Christian soldiers marching as to war—or to any other place we dared to go.

In 1947 at Curtis, 800 boys and girls from kindergarten to Grade 6 were enrolled in the

World-Wide League of Health, the Junior Red Cross. You can still hear them singing their hymn while their voices echo throughout the school:

> We are thy children, Lord,
> Of every race and clime;
> We offer thee a humble gift—
> Our service and our time.

In the autumn of the year, when leaves are falling on the ground and it's getting much colder, you hear excited voices shouting their refrain at the football games:

> C-U-R-T-I-S
> A-C-A-D-E-M-Y
> Are we in?
> Well, I guess.
> Curtis! Curtis!
> Yes! Yes! Yes!

As you look back, you come to recognize the unbeatable quality of your teachers, their kindness, their consideration, and their complete dedication. You even wondered how they could have survived on such paltry wages.

At any rate, you were in love with all your teachers in one way or another: Rowe in French, Andrews in literature, Milley in math, March in history, and Stoodley in chemistry. No one, though, was capable of rendering the kind of teaching Miss Marcella Parsons could afford to give in her seventh grade class.

It was Miss Parsons who gradually brought you out of your painful self-consciousness. She used to say, "Where there's a will there's a way." You loved Longfellow's poem about "a boy's will is the wind's will and the thoughts of youth are long, long thoughts."

Yes, indeed, you fell in love with your teacher, at least, the facsimile of love immaculate, as you were hurled into the depths and glory of academe. You felt you could never succeed without love, passion, and without drive.

Therefore, in reading and writing and in all the other subjects, especially studying for a test, or in memorizing a poem, Miss Parsons provided you with her techniques and inspiration.

You prepared for the quantum leap. At the end of the school year, you could see a smile break over your teacher's face like the sunrise over Signal Hill, when she announced that you had come first in her class.

You were some excited by such wonderful news. Yet, for all that, you wanted to please your teacher rather than gratify yourself in the learning process. Such was the state of the human heart. You concluded all the time that

Miss Parsons was the true champion—you only won the prize.

Elaine Fradsham Luther, a classmate and friend, calls to tell you that the Curtis reunion will take place on Sept. 18, 1999. She came to Curtis from Bay Roberts in 1944. Her fantastic laugh is much the same. Unfortunately she has lost much of her beautiful Bay Roberts' accent.

The drama of the moment is never lost. You will like to see the members o your class of '48 and talk about the old days at Curtis Academy. Priorities lie everywhere. You will celebrate the sense of being and sense of place. As images come to mind, so silence fills the air around you.

There is something, nevertheless, about time and getting older. But there is something fascinating, too, about waking to beat out oblivion any day.

The tableau is fixed forever in your mind. This reunion will be a time to lift up our glasses in a mutual toast to one another.

We will come together and laugh together. Our eyes will shine on a day, a glorious day, the day of red and yellow leaves and faded roses. Then we will come with our delighted faces and our splendid hellos and, later on, we will talk of other adventures yet to be.

ACHOO! ACHOO! ACHOO!

When you cough or sneeze or sniff,
Always use a handkerchief.
(Canadian Red Cross).

The sneeze, the sneeze I can't control;
I know just when it's due;
The sounds come out so stridently:
Achoo! Achoo! Achoo!

The dust, the dust is everywhere,
So I will have to warn you;
My body shakes, my nose erupts:
Achoo! Achoo! Achoo!

When you hear sounds coming through,
Those sounds so loud and clear;
Will dust be the death of me?
Achoo! Achoo! Achoo!

When I am dead and in my grave
And silent as a pew,
No more will you hear my words:
Achoo! Achoo! Achoo!

HIDE-AND-SEEK

When it comes to writing, I get plenty of ideas and then I find I'm being interrupted by so many other images to the point that I don't exactly know if I'm coming or going. It happens with me so often that I carry all those little stories inside my head for years and years without doing anything about them.

I'm always on a journey day after day and, when I get together with my friends, Nick Carew, Cecil Collins, Jim Birmingham, we make everything so exciting. They are dear to me, and we always enjoy each other's company. You will notice what the boys on McKay Street are like, for better or worse, when Mrs. Barnett describes them with her lively verse:

"Something in boys is never stranger,
     never far removed from danger.
Something in boys moves naturally to
     thinnest ice, the tallest tree;
The wildest river, bleakest ridge,
     the deepest wood, the highest bridge.
A boy's restless feet scorn quiet walks,
     swerve into paths of flying rocks;

Leap into ruts, twisting trails,
  courting sharp stones and rusty nails.
Something in boys is never stranger,
  so related to all that danger
That mothers marvel now and then
  how they grow safely into men,
Or wonder, through, some sudden noise,
  if those who did were ever boys."

If it means playing Hide-and-Seek, Hoist your Sails and Run, or any other games, we make a good time of it or stretch it out with marbles for the good part of a day. We are far too busy to be bored, and one thing we never ever have is a chance of being spoiled.

Today is truly one of the most wonderful days of Indian summer on our street. O! The leaves come dancing off the trees, crinkling up as though in the act of dying, but dancing, dancing, swinging and swaying to the music, as more and more leaves continue to fall.

The sun shines brilliantly, birds are singing in the poplar trees, and I sure feel good all over. Above all, I am at peace with myself and my friends. 'Tis sad, too, when you see the nasturtiums in our victory garden looking straggly as they near their end. The sky is extraordinarily blue, and the waves in the harbor rise and fall rhythmically against the gray rocky cliffs.

In Hide-and-Seek, we usually hide ourselves

behind picket fences, in Da Ryan's basement that happens to be unlocked, in a barrel in Mullett's front porch, in O'Brien's hayloft, in McCarthy's ancient garage with its Model T, (its new tires worn out from never having been used on the road), in Jenkins' new house being built on Warbury Street, in the elevator shaft at the Bavarian Brewery, and anywhere else we can think of, if it has any kind of potential for being discovered or never being found.

Suddenly, I have a clever idea. I go to my basement and hide in my Great-Great-Grandfather's (Captain Samuel Wilcox) ancient trunk. For sure, they may never think of looking for me in some old musty trunk. I hop in the trunk and tuck in my head gingerly. As I get in, I close the lid over my head. It is then I hear a click and, it hits me: I may never be found. I must be some kind of bloody fool for having thought of such a crazy idea. That click means one thing to me, that something's wrong somewhere. Talk about being startled. In the beginning my body starts to shake from being locked in this trunk.

That's a fat lot of comfort, isn't it? I know more about the cold chills that run up and down my spine in my summons to death. I am mortally scared and feel like an animal that is stupefied by being caught in a trap. Suddenly I am hot and flustered.

How many times do I keep running my fingers through my hair? My eyes are open, but I see nothing in the pitch-black void. I must try to get used to the anonymous darkness. Yet I am possessed by fear and desire: fear of the threatening predicament, and a desire to discover what life may hold for me.

I get on my back and start kicking the lid with my black-hobnailed boots, but it doesn't give. Then I try to kick at the front of the trunk where the lock is and nothing happens. I know I'm working against time, and I have to do something fast or else resign myself to fate. Now I assume the embryonic state wherein my elbows and hands are placed on the floor. My breathing comes hard. I have been told that a child lives in the eternity of the instant.

The misery of it all is that I'm buried alive in a trunk. Where do I go from here? I'm sweating profusely, and I am also breathing in and breathing out the same stinking foul air of rancid cheese over and over and over again.

The misery of it all takes its toll on me. Inside the trunk, no matter what position I assume, I'm still cramped and can't stretch out for more semblance of comfort. O! Misery me! In a flash I do believe I may lose my life and somehow find it again somewhere. Who knows?

My brain flies off in a tangent, and I hear hysterical sounds. I'm wearing a red plaid shirt and brown corduroy breeks; I'm some uncomfortable for my body is reeking from sweat and urine since the shock of being trapped made me pee. I see a man who continues to stare at me and I ask him,

"Whose funeral is this?"

"You mean to stand there and tell me you don't know whose funeral it is?"

"Look, mister man, would I be asking you if I knew? Give me a break!"

"You old fool! It's your funeral!"

"It is? So what in heaven's name am I doing here talking to you?"

"That's your problem. You have to cope with that yerself."

I know that miserable man, the wretched one, with the gray hair and long nose. He rings a bell with me. He's the weirdo who runs after me every time I go running around the block or to Bowring Park or to Da Parsons for milk, butter, cheese, and eggs.

That same man still gives me the creeps. Every time he follows me, he wields a sharp shiny scythe, so he can adeptly cut off my head, once he catches me. What happens here? As he looks at me slyly, he sneaks up behind and has to make one more step before he gets me; I wake up immediately in my bed in a bath of sweat. Then he asks me,

"Aren't ye goin' to da burial? Ha! Ha!"

"O! I wouldn't miss it for the world."

"Well! More's the pity for ye, snotty guy!"

An odd feeling crosses my mind and carries with it the habit of cynicism that breaks through half-spoken sounds—half-broken words. What a God-forsaken hiding place is this? It vexes me to think that an innocent game of Hide-and-Seek may be futile or even lead to my extinction. Isn't it strange how things can happen in a jiffy? In my brooding moments, I'm afraid that Death Angel will soon blot out the light and life from my weary eyes. Yet in all my wildest dreams, I can't bear to think about the feeling of death. What can I say? I'm absolutely panic-stricken, and there's nothing else I can do but wait.

I'm beside myself and can't stop thinking. It's not such a pleasant thought when it comes to parting with life, especially at a young age, but it only takes a freak accident to happen, and I'm that freak of nature. Surely I can imagine my epitaph may be about my being a holy terror, always getting into fights, and sticking up for my rights, or saying he wasn't rich and he wasn't poor, and as such, he wasn't used to much.

They may see me in a different light with this pronouncement: "You who only see the roughness of his hide, may miss the tenderness of his heart inside." Or he was a believer of sorts, but mostly a believer out of sorts. But as God is my judge, I can read the vivid words summarily engraved upon my tombstone:

"He believed in prayer
And hid in a trunk,
But who would have thunk,
That he'd end up there?"

At least, I'm still breathing the stagnant air and my faculties haven't shut down yet. I suppose by being only 64 pounds, I will make the load much easier for the pallbearers. Now it seems time is imminent, since the end may be near. Who knows? I don't, that's for sure.

Anyway, I'm too young to die. Besides, I'm only halfway through *Wild Horse Mesa* by Zane Grey. John Milton, the British poet, supports my righteous cause, "As good almost kill a man as kill a good book." Therefore, you know the sort of dilemma I'm in. My conscience is my grim reminder: "Watch out! I do believe the dark forces are gaining ground."

I grope in the dark and become weary waiting for something to happen. I shout out at intervals in desperation, "Help me! Help! Help me for God's sake!" The sounds inside the trunk are deafening, but I have to do what needs to be done for it's a matter of life and death.

Of course, I'm a big fan of horror films, and

I am in company with the likes of Bela Lugosi, Lon Chaney, and Count Dracula: they in their crypts, and I in my coffin. What do I see at this moment? A rain-swept old castle, sudden flashes of lightning and constant roars of thunder, and places where hideous giants lurk in the shadows. So the dust and worms aren't the only things that move among the dead. I erase the grim specter of such images from my mind as soon as I can.

The profound sense of despair drives my mind on a swift impulse to seek more wholesome thoughts. I begin to think of love, for I have a crush on Shirley Croucher who tells me she is delighted with the paper valentine I sent her on Valentine's Day. I've been stuck on her for quite awhile. She's the crux of the matter, and the very reason why I want to get out of here. Indeed, Shirley's my girl and I fancy 'tis love that makes the world go 'round. Whenever she looks at me, I get the feeling she goes out with me because she takes pity on me and doesn't want to hurt my feelings. I went out with her last week to a movie, and just as I am to leave, my mother asks me,

"Where are you off to now?"

"O, I'm going out with Shirley again."

She looks at me sternly and says, "Whatever you do, be careful."

"Don't worry. I can take good care of Shirley.

I'm not going to let anyone bother her. That's for sure."

"Remember now, don't go too far!"

"Don't worry. I'm just going to the Nickel Theatre."

"That's not what I mean!"

"I b'lieve I know what you mean, Mom."

We boys never received a great deal in being told about the birds and bees, but we learned about sex bit by bit. We got warmer when we were walking up South River in Bowring Park and saw little white silky balloons drifting aimlessly down the river. We'd pick them up, drain the water out, blow them up, tie each of them up tight, and then slog one another just for the fun of it. Mr. Peter Murphy, the venerable park attendant, comes along and is startled by what he sees, "B'ys! B'y's! What are ye doin'?

My God! What ails ye? Don't put those rubbers in yer mouths. You'll get infected. My Lord, they're 'French Safes' for crying out loud."

We were curious about those so-called balloons, but little did we think that they were germ ridden. Then he told us they were protection against venereal diseases as such:

"Aw! B'y's when ye get older, they can help you, that is, especially, if ye like to wash yer feet with yer socks on."

Somehow I get out of breath just dwelling on Shirley's gorgeous face, when every sigh is a sigh of exclamation. One thing I learn about a girl: if she kisses me, then I'll kiss her back. When it comes to love, I realize you have to read between the lines. Otherwise, it doesn't work. On her paper valentine, I write as neatly as I can: "I love you forever till the day breaks and shadows fly away. Yours truly, Shirley, truly yours, George."

That's my true self coming out. Besides, who wants to walk this blessed earth alone when everything's said and done? It's funny whenever I think of Shirley, I am reminded of a song that was popular when we first met:

"It had to be you; it had to be you.
I wandered around and finally
found somebody who
could make me be true,
could make me be blue
and even be glad just to be sad,
thinkin' of you."

The smell of mothballs is making me gag. Tomorrow I must go to the bakery to play checkers with Mr. Earle. We are tied 1 to 1 and tomorrow's match will be the grand finale. My heart feels like it's leaping into my mouth. This is the worst kind of death: a friend of mine climbs up on the edge of a precipice on Freshwater Bay, surveys the scene below, and dives into the ocean and dies a horrible death.

Unfortunately, there's another grave mistake; the water below was shallower than he thought. It only takes an absent-minded quirk to cause a death. In my mind's eye, I get sick to my stomach when I look at the whole picture before me, along with the grim thought. I may never get to see my family and my friends again. I don't mind being alone once in awhile, but this is ridiculous. My friends probably think I had to go home for some reason or other and may not be aware of such a turn of events.

I hope the mistake I made in getting into a trunk will be a lesson to the small fry. God knows, I've been a good believer, not necessarily the best, but I hardly miss a Sunday School class at Wesley and take time out to study the scriptures and to follow in God's path. I wish to "rejoice with those who rejoice, and weep with those who weep." God sees the predicament I'm in and I have the hope He will get me out of this living hell for blessed is His name:

"In every torment to the heart,
The Lord of Hosts will do His part;
He sympathizes with my grief
And comes to me to bring relief."

Then I push my whole body against the lid with all my might and main, and that doesn't work either. A sense of suffocation assaults me and my body trembles automatically. Then I think if I die, for sure I'd end up somewhere in the midst of the world's mystery, somewhere in heaven or hell for all I know. I'm beginning to smart under such a horrendous ordeal. Life is strange, isn't it? I can manage to hear a train's lone whistle crying out mournfully. Then I'm thinking, "There you are now alive one minute and dead the next."

In the game of Hide-and-Seek, this is one time I want to be found, and sooner the better or else I'll be found dead. In the Bible there is a reference to hide-and-seek. In Isaiah (26:20) I recall these famous words, "Come my people, enter into your chambers, and shut your doors about you: hide yourself for a little moment until the indignation be overpast." Then a prophetic message comes from Matthew (7:7-8): "Ask, and it shall be given you; seek and ye shall find; knock and it shall be opened unto you: For everyone who asks, receives; and he who seeks, finds; and to him who knocks it shall be opened."

Words of a hymn come to my lips from "The Hymnary (Copyright, Canada, 1930, by the United Church Publishing House)":

> "The King of Love my shepherd is
> Whose goodness faileth never;
> I nothing lack if I am His,
> And He is mine forever."

I cry out for help and reflect on Psalm 30:5, when David praises God for his deliverance and exhorts others to praise Him: "For His anger endures but a moment; in His favor is life: weeping may endure for a night, but joy comes in the morning."

I am breathing heavily and my heart is beating rapidly against my rib cage—more rapidly than ever before in all my life. In fact, my rib cage is sore from the continuous beating it takes from the heart. "O, God! If you're for real, now is the time to prove yourself!"

I'm so crowded in here in such stark darkness; it sure looks like I'm being laid out not in a trunk but in a coffin. Will I ever live again? Will this eternal silence never end? I think of death, and since I'm a Christian, why should I have any fear of death in the final analysis?

I'm beginning to look for some kind of compromise since I do believe I'm nearing the end. I'm beginning to get the drift of things, for I believe if I die and make it to heaven, I may have a good chance to see my cousins, my grandparents, and a lot of my friends who died suddenly.

I always believe God listens to prayers and He knows that if my prayers come from the heart, He will in His great kindness and condescending way, save me in any kind of danger. Of course, when Jesus was on earth, people asked Him, "What shall we do so we might work the works of God?" Jesus answered and said unto them, "This is the work of God, that ye believe in Him whom He has sent."

All of us young ones believe God reigns and rules in the universe while the Devil gnashes his teeth with sudden rage for, if he could get away with it, he would tear God from His throne in an instant.

The air I breathe is running scarce and my heart is pumping madly; even my mind is being worn out by grief. I have only one person to blame for getting me into such a trying situation: me. I just have to wait and wait and keep on waiting. So this trunk is my coffin and this coffin is my waiting room and I'm waiting in this waiting room; what for, waiting for death?

In the name of God, I can't believe that the Devil is waiting for me somewhere in the void. I get hotter and hotter just thinking about the actual fear of my own destiny. My efforts to breathe are getting to be more painful for I'm running out of air and I'm running out of time.

In spite of such a frightening experience, I linger for awhile on a venerable Psalm I learned at Wesley: "He heals the broken in heart, and binds up his wounds. He tells the number of the stars; He calls them all by their names.

Great is our Lord, and of great power: His understanding is infinite." (Psalms 147:3-5).

"Help me Jesus! Looka here! If you're worth your salt, then you should get here pretty soon or else I'll be a dead duck." Then I shout out to the top of my lungs and wonder if there's anyone around who can hear my cries for help.

I realize it's good to be humble, especially when you're down and out as it were; I find there's no end to the mysteries of life and death. The air is foul in this place. I may seem tired and fagged out, but I must never give up hope. No siree! Believe you me, I'm in quest of "The Peace which passes understanding." Yes! I'm some exhausted; I hope all my efforts have not been in vain.

Being lost is the same as being buried alive, or lost in the wilderness or lost at sea. I am, though, still alive, but I still have some patience left to endure the hard knocks and disappointments in life. Let me tell you, I need to be rescued, but if I should die here, I may yet find salvation in ways that are not known to me.

Therefore, all I know is from my experience along with the faith that tells me, if I survive, then you, the reader, may profit from such an experience. I still hear some well-chosen words from Reverend Armitage's sermon:

"If your cry is heartfelt, and if you feel that you have been defeated in your efforts, then your cry will be answered. You may also learn a little about the psychology of life. If you have suffered from phobias, from panic attacks, from fear of being lost, then God will return to heal your wounds. This is God, God the Father, the God of Love. He is the same God to whom we pray in the watches of the night. So remember, when you come to pray, God will help the wandering soul that yearns for Him."

That clicking sound will stay with me always. I recognize the sickening gloom and doom of it. The sweat keeps rolling down from my black smudgy eyebrows. Again I still keep kicking my feet against the lid of the trunk—to no avail. There's no escape because the trunk is solidly constructed. I envision being taken out dead and then I can see the woman, the mid-wife, Mrs. Jones, who takes care of baby deliveries, and on the side, waxes on and waxes off the corpses who have recently died. I'm dying to hear the sounds of my friends who are saying, "We found him in a trunk in his basement behind the furnace."

Notwithstanding, the doubts about survival and its chilling endeavor, and having reflected on my condition, I do want the reader to be fully assured of my fidelity. My lips are dry and I'm running out of air and my mind is working overtime. I shudder, though, to believe I'm going to die in a freak accident like this; then again, this is not the first time someone smothered in a trunk.

I know in my heart of hearts that I want to live more than anything in the world. On the other hand, I realize the grim reality of being at death's door in this coffin. How long have I been here? It sure feels like an eternity. I am both scared and ashamed of what I have done just for the sake of a little game.

I begin to figure I am not long for this world since my days are numbered as sad as it is to say such a thing. Suddenly, I hear another click and it appears to be a door opening. Am I just thinking this? Or is it a delusion?

Sure enough I hear footsteps on the concrete floor and those steps keep coming. Those same repetitive sounds are on their way up the basement stairs. Suddenly they stop on the stairway.

Unfortunately, I am too weak to shout out, but with my bunched-up fist, I keep knocking in steady strokes on the walls of the trunk. I'm at a fever-pitch at this moment, for I'm being caught somewhere between fear and hope. I begin to hear the steps and they are getting closer.

No one has to tell me about life. I fool myself when I tell others I'm doing well, but I am much more hopeful than ever before. Unexpectedly, the lid of the trunk opens. It's my mother, but I'm too exhausted to move.

She sees my limp body, bends over the trunk, and puts her arms around me, and then lifts me up from the trunk and shrieks out, "What in Heaven's name are you doing in there?"

I have no answer. I am much too weak to speak and far too gone to walk. My mother carries me as if I'm a sack of potatoes up the basement stairs and lays me down on the black couch in the kitchen.

I look at my mother and catch my breath with a word or two, "Mom! You saved my life! I can't believe it! I was on my last legs and now I'm alive on such a day as this." Such an escapade is so astounding that there is no feeling to which it can be compared in my lifetime. In retrospect, I learn that I had a panic attack, a real one and not imagined, for I have a terrible dread of my cramped environment, shortness of breath, rapid heart rate, trembling, shaking, and sweating. Actually, I believed for sure I was going to die or else go out of my mind, as it were, in the horror of being trapped. I may add, I've always been claustrophobic, and this attack didn't help matters.

This scary event happened during the troubled times of the Second World War. You see, when I hear a beautiful war song we used to sing, it carries more significance for me now. The words and sounds are quite soothing: "WHEN THE LIGHTS GO ON AGAIN ALL OVER THE WORLD."

"As you know, son, I planned to go downtown this morning, but it was a good thing I didn't. Thank God for that!"

"Mom!! When did you think there was something the matter?"

"I thought the sounds I heard were those made by the cat, but when I heard the knocking, I realized there was something radically wrong. Well, I never! Why would you hide in a trunk, above all?"

"It seemed logical at the time. Now I realize how absurd it was after the fact. I never could believe such a thing like this would ever happen to me." I thought for sure you were going to say to me, "Fancy meeting you here!" Or, "Did I catch you at a bad time?"

"When I saw you in such a terrible state, I knew this was not the time to be funny. One look at you and I could tell you were in a bad way."

"Mom! You're as good as gold! I don't know what I would have done without you. All I can say is I owe you my life."

In retrospect, my mother usually goes down our pathway once a day to Warbury Street, south of our street, to check on my great-grandmother, Jessie Caroline Wilcox Cassidy, and her daughter, Elizabeth Hillier. Fortunately, my mother came by in the nick of time and saved my life for which I am most grateful.

It's ironic, too, that my mother won the game of Hide-and-Seek that day. Ever since my rescue I am so grateful to God and so happy to be alive.

THE RIDE OF MY LIFE

I leave my house and I see Mr. John Collins standing beside his horse and four-wheeled wagon on McKay Street. He is the congenial neighbour and veteran driver for Norwood Lumber Company.

"Hello, Mr. Collins! Are you off to work?"

"Yes, me b'y! If it's a lift you're after wantin', hop right on!"

"That'll be nice, sir! Thank you."

When I take a look at the horse, I am mindful of a book I read about, *Wild Horse Mesa* by Zane Grey. I see the driver's horse as the perfect specimen with its massive muscles and commanding height; for sure it's mighty compelling to any child's eye.

Mr. Collins is married to his wife, Bridie, and is a hard working man for all that. Their son, Patrick, a handsome strapping young man, is currently fighting with the Newfoundland 166th regiment somewhere in France.

Usually, though, Mr. Collins is a quiet man, but once in awhile, I get the impression from him that he would like to go back to his roots in Ireland and visit the old homestead.

The reader can surely understand the homesickness many Newfoundlanders endure in trying to return to Ireland: its scenic beauty, its ancient monuments, and historic sites. In this man's longing, he tells me he'd like to visit his relatives who are still living there—to see the old castles, to listen to all kinds of stories and yarns, and come to a pub where the Guinness flows down your throat like liquid silk.

You get a lump in your throat when he talks about that sort of stuff that brings tears to your eyes. Mr. Collins's son is Dick whose sons, in turn, are Jack, Cec, and Billy or more familiarly known as "Boof." Years later, before he died, Mr. Collins tells me that his people came from a place near Cork, Ireland, and that he was related to a Michael Collins who happened to be one of the greatest heroes that Ireland ever produced. "In fact," he says, "this man had his last drink in a little place called Bealnablath. Actually, truth to tell, he was shot at and killed north of this same place; too bad for he was only 32 years old at the time."

Years later, I found Mr. Collins' facts were authentic, for there was a Michael Collins who was born in the small village of Woodfield just south of Bealnablath in the year 1890. Indeed, he was a soldier, patriot, and politician in Irish affairs. He used to be the leader of Sinn Fein and did his part in negotiating the 1921 treaty that firmed up the present boundary lines between Northern Ireland and the Republic itself. Unfortunately, he was killed in 1922.

By the same token, Bridie keeps busy every day and even takes pity on the beggar man. She is busy doing something or other like washing clothes, darning socks, knitting sweaters, saving crocks when she makes jams, and doing everything to make her husband happy all the while. She even makes the beggar man feel at home with the occasional home-cooked dinner. I hope, though, she doesn't spoil him with all her generosity.

My friends are Nick and John Carew, Bob Shaw, Jim Birmingham, and Cec Collins. They are bazzing marbles to the mot in front of Power's House on McKay Street. I wave to them and they wave back. I tell them, "I'll see you guys later."

Mr. Collins takes out his pipe and Prince Albert tobacco, lights up, and, together, we're on our way along the graveled street towards our journey. There's something pleasant and reassuring about the casual pace in our world with the horse's trot, trot, trot.

On the right side of the street, I wave to Mr. Danny Delmar Donnelley who is on his way to work at City Service. He is father of Eileen, and Claude and Dan, who are fraternal twins only seven minutes apart.

Their mother and father are actors in plays

on the stage in the city. Danny Delmar, I must remind you, is a brilliant man—the wizard who has the gift of prophecy.

I remember Dan telling me about the song his father wrote when he had Adolf Hitler in mind. The song speaks for itself:

> "O, you nasty Nazi man
> way over in Berlin.
> You don't have a blinkin' chance
> this blimey war to win.
> We'll take our Charlie Chaplin
> and put him 'neath your chin
> and if that don't do, a buckeroo,
> but we'll get you in Berlin."

This is the song for the whole world to hear. When we listen to the wizard's magical words, a fierce note of pride comes into the heart of every Newfoundlander. In retrospect, as the sun comes out brilliantly on our street, it seems like blasphemy to dwell on war.

As soon as we get to Warbury Street, my mind works overtime because my great-grandmother, Jessie Caroline Wilcox Cassidy, and her daughter, Elizabeth Hillier, live at 36 Warbury Street. We hear there's always a solid woman behind a good man. In my case, I can honestly say, behind a boy, there is a mother and her daughter who make my day every day of every single year.

From them I learn a lot about the Holy Bible and the strangeness of the Trinity: Father, Son, and Holy Ghost. At my early age, though, I find it so difficult with the concept that God is not only one person, but He is incorporated into three bodies. Yet I follow my principles in learning from no other book except the Bible.

Where else can you find the principles of love so fully expressed in Leviticus 19:18?

"Thou shalt not avenge, nor bear any grudge against the children of thy people, but thou shalt love thy neighbour as thyself: I am the Lord."

Where else can you find forgiveness? When Christ appears before us to say He will "open their eyes, and to turn them from darkness to light, and from the power of Satan unto God, that they may receive forgiveness of sins, and inheritance among them which are sanctified by faith that is in me."

Where else can you find peace except in the Psalms? We find the love for God's word brings to us our peace of mind in Psalm 119:165-168.

"Great peace have they which love thy law: and nothing shall offend them. Lord, I have hoped for thy salvation, and done thy commandments. My soul hath kept thy testimonies; and I love them exceedingly. I have kept thy precepts and thy testimonies: for all thy ways are before me."

Jessie Cassidy lived during Abraham Lincoln's Presidency, and when I look at her, I become an integral part of the American Civil War. She reads me a message about Lincoln writing a letter to a Mrs. Bixby. When she was finished reading, I was overwhelmed by the heartfelt emotions expressed by the president. I kept that same letter with me for over 60 years and pasted it in my Caribou Scribbler in 1943. This is the president's letter in its entirety:

"Executive Mansion, Washington, November 21, 1864.

Mrs. Bixby, Boston, Massachusetts:

Dear Madam: I have been shown in the files of the War Department a statement of the Adjutant-General of Massachusetts that you are the mother of five sons who have died gloriously on the field of battle. I feel how weak and fruitless must be any words of mine which should attempt to beguile you from the grief of a loss so overwhelming. But I cannot refrain from tendering to you the consolation that may be found in the thanks of the Republic they died to save. I pray that our Heavenly Father may assuage the anguish of your bereavement, and leave you only the cherished memory of the loved and lost, and the solemn pride that must be yours to have laid so costly a sacrifice upon the altar of freedom.

Yours very sincerely and respectfully,

Abraham Lincoln"

Before we get to Leslie Street, the unpardonable thing happens. I observe magnanimous swishing of the horse's shiny black tail from one side to another until it stops. Then it happens: the hot oats or what we call "ocky poo" keeps spurting out from the horse's rear end. You've seen it before. The odour is as raunchy as it can possibly be. You brace yourself when the horrible wind dilates your nostrils.

As the horse trots down Leslie Street, just beyond Warbury Street, I see Jack Baird's Barber Shop. I was there early last Saturday morning for a haircut. Anyway, when I open the door, I can hear the strident tones of three men laughing while Jack is cutting hair.

A middle-aged man is reading the *Daily News* and he laughs out exuberantly, "Hey, Jack! It says in this here paper that the British housewives are refusing to take it on their backs anymore." For all that, I don't believe I got the whole story.

Indeed, I become quite curious. As soon as I get home, I rush to speak to my mother, "Hey, Mom! These men were in the barbershop and they were laughing about the fact that the British housewives are not going to take it on their backs anymore. Can you tell me why they were laughing?"

I soon recognize a big laugh on my mother's face. Shortly after, she says, "Never mind, son! There's probably more to it than meets the eye."

As we lumber down the street, Mr. Collins holds the reins a little tighter because of the steepness of this hill; he guides the horse so he can watch out for the dips and turns that call for more cautious trotting.

Just below I recognize on the left is the home where my wonderful third grade teacher, Miss Jean White, lives. This woman helps me so much with my reading and, generally speaking, she makes my life worthwhile. As a rule, teachers are never absent from Centenary Hall School, but the other day, Miss White must have been the exception. After school is out, I run towards her home and stop stock still at her door. After all, she is the one who helps me so much in putting my life together.

I ring the doorbell and the mother comes to the door. "Yes? What brings you here today?"

"O! I'm Miss White's pupil, and I'm just wondering how she's making out. Is she sick? Or what?"

"I understand. Do come in and take your clothes off."

"Thank you, missus."

Miss White comes downstairs and seems to have brightened up when she sees me. "I came, Miss White, since I'm concerned. Are you all right?"

"Thank you, Mr. Hillier, for remembering me. I have a cold, but I will be back in school tomorrow. Make no mistake about it."

I also give her a handful of buttercups from a meadow in Thompson's Field, and she appears most grateful for the thought.

I notice she's holding a white hanky in her hand; occasionally, she brings the hanky to her lips and coughs up some of the sputum that is readily absorbed by the hanky.

Mrs. White has me sit at the dining room table. Then we have tea together except I am drinking a tumbler of lemon crystals. I have been given excursion bread that's so appetizing, especially if you're going on a journey or excursion. Both mother and daughter thank me for coming by. In retrospect, it may seem weird to believe that my heart is getting so sentimental towards my teacher. Jeepers! I can hardly stand the separation between Miss White and myself.

We are almost at the bottom of the hill, but on the left side of the street, Mrs. Thompson is getting dolled up to go shopping on Water Street. She looks in the mirror matter-of-factly.

As she spruces herself up, she powders her nose and dabs on lipstick and a little rouge.

She is a beautiful woman, but everything happens in a jiffy. To her shock and distress, the mirror smashes into smithereens before her very eyes. She is beside herself and calls her husband at work.

Evidently, Mr. Skinner, the next-door neighbour, was cleaning his six-shooter, and the gun went off. Erratically, the bullet pierced through the side of the Thompson's clapboard house with sufficient force to smash the mirror in her bedroom.

Mr. Skinner was most apologetic and told Mrs. Thompson not to take it personally. This man is the owner of a successful firm in the city, "Skinner's Marbleworks." It's interesting to know that one of Mr. Skinner's customers bought a monument for his lovely wife just in case of the grave possibility she might die. After having waited for more than a year, he got some disgusted because she hadn't even used it yet.

Another woman on the street is terribly ill and tries to get her husband to understand her dire circumstances. Nevertheless, Mr. Skinner goes along with his business of inscribing the message on her monument. As usual, having tried to convince her husband that she was hurting, she was exasperated with him.

Summarily, she dies, and he goes off to the General Protestant Cemetery to pay his last respects. He stands solemnly beside her grave, and as soon as he reads the epitaph, he almost has an apoplectic fit. It says in boldface print: "I TOLD YOU I WAS SICK!"

I must also tell you that near Shortall's house, I see Jack Rabbitts come by, riding up Leslie Street on a beautiful black stallion. He looks mighty resplendent in all his glory. On the contrary, we are at war, and here is a man who should have joined up to support its cause. So, in a manner of reproof and sharp urgency, I call out to him loud and clear, "Slacker! Slacker you! Why dontcha j'ine up?"

With the same, it's as if I stopped him dead in his tracks. He turns around and memorizes every particle of my face. I am petrified for the moment, but I get my licks in. Yet, during those troubled times, he must have donated more blood to help in the war effort than any man in the whole wide world.

Even when I get to summer camp with the Church Lads Brigade, I meet him once more. I am in a wheelbarrow race in Topsail Camp grounds, and Harry Simmons, an orphan boy from Bay Roberts, is holding my legs. All I have to do is paw at the ground before me in order to get to the finish line.

Unfortunately, my thumb must've been cut

by a piece of glass. I am taken to the first aid tent and there is Jack Rabbitts tending on the infirmed. When he sees me, I know he hasn't forgotten me. He has a scowl on his face, "What do you want?"

"Can't you see the blood dripping from my thumb?" I must say, though, he was an expert at everything he did. I daresay he could have been a doctor if he had put his mind to it. When he patches me up, I am most grateful and say, "Thank you very much, Bunny Rabbitts!"

A ride is a ride, but when it's a ride on the cobblestones of Water Street, that's something different. The half-buried cobbles are dreadfully efficient. Anyway, my curiosity, no doubt, has suddenly been aroused by a few suspicions taking shape in the back of my mind. I get a much tighter grip on the splintered plank I'm sitting on, beside a load of matchboard.

There's not much freedom on a Spartan bed. Instinctively, I am presently an inheritor of Saint Vitus Dance. The brazen, distinctive whip creates occasional silver shadows on the horse's hide.

My feet dangle in the air as the iron wheels revolve convulsively. The very thought I may fall off the wagon petrifies me momentarily. Just because I'm paranoid doesn't mean the world is not out to get me. I can hear the constant rattle of the metal wheels against the hard impenetrable stones. On this street we belong to the lower class, but the only essential difference between the lower and upper is that the lower class has a fixed income while the upper is fixed for life.

The ride rocks me up and down just as if I'm on a schooner coming up on the crest of a wave and then sinking hard again into the hollows. Each bump gives me a jolt worse than the one before. My Spartan seat gets harder and harder. I move my backside a little for some sense of relief.

Of course, my indomitable pluck and high spirit will never admit that I want to call it a day. Obviously, the driver and I are surrounded by motor cars. These cars are nothing but impostors, turning into fighting bulls, ready to lock horns, and unwilling to give us any ground so to speak. It's much like we're not worth our salt anymore.

One driver is impatient and shouts out, "Get off the street! You don't belong! The horse and cart are obsolete!" Mr. Collins scowls at the drivers and spits tobacco juice into the furtive autumn air. Some motorists laugh at us, the kind of laugh that brings shivers down your spine. Although you get the picture about the inevitability of change, you still loathe the artificial atmosphere as well as the continuous noise and rancid smell of those motor cars.

In the twinkling of an eye, I blurt out at the driver who is blowing his horn at us, "I know your horn works! Now try your brakes! Sir! I hope you get four flats including your spare!"

When we get to Horwood Lumber Company, I thank the driver, "Thank you, Mr. Collins. I appreciate the lift." He responds by winking at me, "You're welcome. Anytime, me old trout!"

I pick up a hat for my mother at a milliner's on Water Street East. On my way out the store, I am intrigued by what the young female clerk is saying to a lady,

"You're a good customer of hours, Mrs. Pearce, and we wants you to be 'appy by hall means. The howner what keeps the 'at shop said 'ow the 'at wasn't come back has of yet. She said a young liddy bought it yestiddy hafternoon and hasked to 'ave it sent to you this morning afore the noonday gun goes hoff."

I do believe the English cockney accent and the Bay Roberts one remain synonymous. Hime sure there's a distinctive link between the two. I tease Elaine Fradsham, who 'ails from Bay Roberts, habout 'er haccent, but to tell the truth, she speaks hit so sonorously that hit will stay with me forhever hafter.

IT'S A CHILD'S
CHRISTMAS AFTER ALL

Nature reigns when the earth turns white
And the wind moans its worst at night.
Poetry is winter. Look at
That wind whip around your corner
Like a wicked metaphor. The chill
Touches the heart of your being.
Look at the sky with its leaden
Adjectives. The snow performs its
Unjust deeds. Snow—you will never
Escape from it—soft, leaping, cruel.
Time leans heavily upon you.
Yet everything belongs to you
This Christmas: bolder requests for
Peace on Earth, thoughts of permanence,
Of roots, of quiet words on giving
And receiving. Now you're older,
Doesn't your own child-like wonder
Still stir deep within as you
Dwell on Bethlehem and the
Recurring dream? Suddenly, you
Feel as if some missing part of you
Has just slid into place, making
You complete. So, where are you now?

O, there! After the babble of
Conversation has just died down,
There you are, of course, a witness
To the elegiac silence.

A CHILD'S CHRISTMAS IN NEWFOUNDLAND

Christmas marks a glorious beginning for you. The truth begins like a bell in your mind and heart and soul, pealing forth the magnificence of the birth of a Child—the most loving one who ever walked upon the face of the earth.

In the eye of the mind, the past is present. Christmas comes and the heart returns to the place where you were born. December comes down from the mountains in a white fury and locks the valley of Saint John's into its icy grip. Waterford River comes to a frozen stop. You have not forgotten the sense of it all, not even in the stubborn silence.

Snow falls softly on Thompson's Field as you and your friends ski down the hill with your waxed barrel staves and broom-handle sticks. You can hardly see ahead of you; your hot breath trails after you.

Mundy pond is frozen and snow-covered, and gravel roads are hard-packed, and the trees around McKay Street look mighty black, cold, and brittle. It doesn't matter, though, for the stage is already set. When December comes along, you are as good as you can be.

It's wartime, 1940, and it's Christmas Eve, and you're selling your *Evening Telegram*s on Water street near the Red Rose Cafe. You have your pitch fully rehearsed, "Gear up! Derry up! Tel-uh-gear-ee-yam!" You don't know what the slogan means, but it seems to work for you.

Your pitch changes with its Yuletide twist, "Merry Christmas! Happy New Year! Tel-uh-gear-ee-yam! See my paper! Buy my paper! Tel-uh-gear-ee-yam!" Now you are near Ayre & Sons big department store, and you can't help but listen to the old Christmas Carol being played softly on the street:

> "God rest you merry gentlemen,
> Let nothing you dismay;
> Remember Christ our Savior
> Was born on Christmas Day.
> To save us all from Satan's power
> When we were gone astray;
> O tidings of comfort and joy,
> Comfort and joy,
> O tidings of comfort and joy!"

It doesn't matter where you go to church, if it's at Gower or Wesley or Cochrane Street United Church or St. Mary's or St. Patrick's; your hopes are always being entertained at Christmas time by the old familiar splendor.

It's Christmas Eve, and you are in the presence

of Canon Stirling showing Lantern Slides at St. Mary's on Southside Road. He has a pointer, and he tells you about Jesus and the poignant meaning of a gift; the gift is what you fall for, a God-given gift of love beyond something corporeal.

When Canon Stirling taps his pointer adroitly upon the canvas floor, his worthy assistant shows you a snap of Gabriel, the archangel, one of the seven holy angels, who comes down from heaven on swiftest wing and appears before the Blessed Virgin.

You absorb the news about the joyful tidings that Mary herself shall conceive and bear a Son immaculately. Although Mary waxes great, she is sort of afraid. The canon tells you the absolute truth of it all: the Son, appointed God of life and love itself on Christmas Day.

It's Midnight Mass and you are now at St. Patrick's Church with Nick, and Cec, and Jim. You feel out of place, for this is not your church where another kind of God lives.

The white candles burn low and make the stained glass windows glow. While you're there, you're still believing in the grandeur of God's light while your spirit soars to undreamed-of heights, and truth permeates your mortal being. Bells ring twelve to break the holy silence— that kind of silence which belongs in a church.

You hear a soprano's voice from the throat

of Newfoundland's own, Julie Andrews, who is singing *Ave Maria*, and the insides of your stomach begin to cry out in delight. It's like you want to rise on wings and become imbued with the mystery of God's power.

The Mass is over, and your tongue gets stuck in the roof of your mouth. You cross yourself the same way that Nick, Cec, and Jim do, and you return home in the darkness of the cold, winter's night and feel as if you've just been sanctified, for you honestly believe that death and darkness are no more.

You've been happy most of the time, but now winter's voice is about loneliness, since you are getting sentimental. You think of the past and loved ones on Christmas Day. But one thing is certain; you are not afraid to die, even though, for a while, you thought you'd be the worst coward in Christendom.

You rise to the tender mercy of time. You try to hold on to something like a holy tradition. As a faithful believer, you look into the mirror to see who is who. You begin to wonder, "Who is who, and by the way, who are you?"

In the shadowed light, Christmas comes again, and you are pleased with all your heart. There is nothing like birth. There is nothing like love. Then, too, there is nothing like the silence of snow falling down upon your street.

Christmas is love, eye-to-eye, and face-to-face,

family, friends, relatives, a stocking filled with an apple, an orange, grapes, nuts, and candies, a gift getting ready to excite you, a decorated tree sparkling in the corner of a room, and a dressed-up turkey roasting in the oven.

Though you miss the opportunity of watching your flocks at night, you grope through the yielding world of hazy contours, vague surfaces, and capricious depths. You somehow never forget a just and noble cause. You still sing Christmas carols for the sake of love and praise.

The Reverend Armitage is your minister at Wesley United Church, and it is Christmas time when he centers on the mind of Jesus Christ and his message about peace and fortitude. We are the minister's sheep; we are his flock, and he is our good shepherd.

You used to call your minister, "Holy One," and as far as you remember, he never told you it was otherwise. His voice lifts up the congregation, "And it came to pass in those days" as he turns your world into a merry-go-round. Your wish is to follow the star in the East. Impatiently, you utter to yourself, "Who does Caesar Augustus think he is, anyway? That bloody nuisance!"

You get into the swing of things as you visualize shepherds telling their own stories and angels singing in praise of love beneath the brilliant heavens.

Your minister tells you that when the child is born, the sun leaps up into the heavens, stars dance and stream out, and night turns to day.

Peace comes to every mountain, stream, and forest, and God is now active in your world. There is nothing to worry about. So you give up most of your own unproductive thinking and affirm your faith in Jesus Christ.

The old Christmases were simpler then—just simpler and more natural. You were also caught up in your belief in Santa Claus who would come to find your place on Christmas Eve. And what a constant thrill as you lie in bed in winter, steeped in wonder. You are filled with lyrical stirrings. There goes the missed heartbeat—one moment's gap in being. Images keep reeling in your brain:

"Jolly old Saint Nicholas
Lean your ear this way;
Don't you tell a single soul
What I'm going to say:
Christmas Eve is coming soon;
Now you dear old man,
Whisper what you'll bring to me,
Tell me if you can."

You begin to wonder why a hockey stick is in your mother's bedroom closet. You are afraid to look out into the heavens, afraid you'll see a mass of moving colors. The scene hypnotizes you, infusing your every sense. There you are with suspended breath and half-closed eyes till sleep becomes the compromise.

Of course, you believe, your Santa will come, that cumbrous figure in red, streaking across the night sky to find your place. Now that you are older, doesn't your child-like wonder still stir deep within you, so memory opens its eyes for the sake of Bethlehem and the recurring dream?

A TOUGH COMPETITOR
AND A GOOD MAN

A local sports legend, Dunc Sharpe, was really tough only on himself.

Out of the dim and discerning past, I remember you, Dunc Sharpe, from the early 50s. In late August, I read the local sports briefs in the *Telegram* and saw, "Tough competitor dead at 65." I felt stunned by the news. I look to the past for answers. Yes, you were some tough, but you were always kind to me.

Indeed, you may have been the toughest. For sure, you wouldn't have been Dunc Sharpe if you didn't get your Irish up. Besides, whatever else was there to do? Why would you wish to be a clone of someone else?

In track, your specialty was the 440-yard run during Sports Day on Bell Island. I watched you knuckle under by doing your jumping jacks. I saw the look of intent in your eyes. Your appearance was glum, yet you set about your goal instantly for the inevitable moment of reckoning.

The competitors were lined up, the gun went off, and at that self-same instant, things flashed in your head. You went all out and sprinted 300 yards, and then, for the rest of the race, you made it on sheer guts.

In fact, you made sure you utilized your last breath before you crossed the finish line. Then, having won, you fell, full-face forward, exhausted on the grass. Finally, you caught your breath.

Yes, you were the toughest one and the hardest on yourself. There is no question in my mind, under the proper techniques of coaching, you may have turned into a world-record-beater in this event with your rapid strides and your body's motion.

"Dunc Sharpe, one of the fiercest competitors in St. John's sports history, is dead," said the article in the *Telegram*. You disproved the outlook on things about the meek inheriting the earth.

Yes, I dare say, you may have been the fiercest competitor of all. But, of course, years ago, we all carried parochial gods on our backs.

You, Len Coughlan, Grant Chalker, and I were proud to represent Newfoundland in the Inter-Provincial Track Meet in Toronto on Sept. 4, 1953, as a tune-up for the coming Olympic training competitions at the Canadian National Exhibition.

Newfoundland fans praised us on our way, for we were some keen on running the greatest race of our lives against stiff competition up along, all in our quest for the Holy Grail.

At this moment, I'm writing my tribute to Dunc in the public library dedicated to none other than Dr. A. C. Hunter. I stare into Professor Hunter's face, and as soon as I see his photograph, the past returns.

We had him in English for Milton's *Areopagitica* and John Stuart Mill's *On Liberty.* Once the bell rang for the end of the period, we rushed to the French doors, but on this specific day Dr. Hunter got there before us.

He held up his hand in protest, stopped us in our tracks, stared into our faces, and intoned with his impeccable dialect, "Hold it right 'theah'—I have yet another pearl to 'cawst.'" Aw, but, he was dedicated to his teaching and marked strictly along English lines.

"The former, St. John's city engineer died Sunday. He was 65," said the article in the paper. Dunc Sharpe was a productive thinker and his grades in engineering at MUN were excellent. Unfortunately, the last time I saw him was 45 years ago.

"A hard-nosed St. Bon's athlete," the story said, "Sharpe participated in hockey, soccer, and track and field during the 1950s."

Len Coughlan, one of the unsung heroes of city sports, reminded me, also, that Dunc was a fantastic rower at Quidi Vidi on Regatta Day.

"George," he said, "Dunc was the difference when it came to winning. You should have seen the gigantic swirls he made when his oar touched the water. Only Dunc could have been that determined."

Grant Chalker told me, "Dunc put his nose to the grindstone in every track and field event. That sure made him hard-nosed. In the '50s, he was impossible to beat, especially in the 440." Most of the time, Dunc was shy and non-confrontational, but he avenged himself on the battlefield. Once I watched him play soccer for Stan Carew's Engineers' versus Georgie Hickman's "Bay Boys." They may have been bay boys, but they were superior students who carried their own "message to Garcia" at MUC and MUN (Memorial University College and Memorial University Newfoundland.)

The match was played on the old pitch off Parade Street. When Dunc kicked the ball in the air, he always woke up God. He was menacing, too, especially in that brouhaha between himself and Walter Cull, mister five-by-five, and powerfully built. Wow! For sure, that soccer match was bloody war to claim a desperately-earned championship. Dunc always put his best foot forward, so to speak. Of that we can be sure. Wow again!

Somewhere in Matthew, we are reminded that Peter was able in a sense to walk on water, that is, once he focused his energies on Jesus Christ.

Undoubtedly, Dunc never walked on water, but when he played hockey for St. Bon's, he flew over ice. He was on the defense team for St. Bon's when they won the Boyle Challenge Cup Trophy for four years ending in 1959. Other members on defense were Noel Hutton, Len Coughlan, and Joe Slaney.

It's too bad we had only one track meet a year. No one could surpass Dunc Sharpe, for he was so determined to win, unencumbered by any fear or circumstance.

We were all so impressed with his speed, versatility, his guts, and glory. He was a track and field team unto himself—Jim Thorpe on the Rock. Indeed, he was "Victor Ludorum Dunc." Didn't we have fun, though, at the Highland Games in Antigonish, when we watched Tink Kyte high-jumping for the Halifax Wanderers, and the sweet, young lassies doing the Highland Fling? You could hear the calculated chuckles and giggles from the young women as they watched big, brutish highlanders tossing their cabers, not unlike telephone poles, to make manifest their perfect selves.

Our spirits, Dunc, were lifted up by your efforts as we proclaimed peace to one another at Corpus Christi Church on Waterford Bridge Road.

The thought of death dissolves before our

very eyes. We hear its plaintive tones. We know nothing about the hereafter, but there is something inside us no power on earth can dissolve because it is right and proper to believe a mountain is meant to be climbed, not just because it's there, but upon reaching the summit, heaven touches the sky.

This is our hope. This is our identity. So, at last, William Duncan Sharpe, on this moment we are justified by saying, "We loved you, man!"

THE DAY I RACED
THE STREETCAR

In the winter, when icicles hang down from Southside Hills, the hard frozen street turns into a hockey rink. I remember the sharp night frosts of December: my friends and their fine faces freezing in the cold, the squalls of snow, bung eyes from the snowball fights, and the bumpers, giant marshmallows that we rolled down the hills.

Now the long submerged spring emerges, and the roots of the city return to life. Soon Thompson's Field will be a buttercup meadow and Ayre's Woods a forest green.

At the end of the street I smell the hops coming from the huge outside tank at Bavarian Brewery. I then walk leisurely down Leslie Street and look upon the Southside Hills. When the fog and drizzle set in, the hills are black, but when the day is as bright as a stained-glass window, the hills turn a beneficent blue.

Leslie is not a street; it's a hill, far hillier than most hills I have ever encountered. I call Leslie Street, on its way up to the Higher Levels, a vasomotor tune-up for any Cassius with that lean and hungry look.

Halfway down Leslie, I pass the house where a beautiful girl lives. When I look at the house I get the goose bumps and lose my voice, since a frog gets stuck in the middle of my throat. She attends Prince of Wales College and is older than I. Yet I am in love with her.

I remember when she smiled at me once, and I melted off the face of the earth. I am mesmerized by the process of adoration. I still see the flawless skin, the chestnut curls, and eyes of unforgettable luster. This is the time when I fell in love, the time when I got to believe in the Creator for creating such an angel. One time I wrote a poem about her; these are some of the lines I recall:

> I feel such redness in my face
> And show some signs of guilt,
> But from the corner of my eye, I say,
> "I love the way you're built."

Standing beside Norris's fence at the corner of Leslie and Water Streets, I wait patiently for the streetcar to run down from Big Brown's, the family grocery at the Crossroads. The peoples' faces and gestures are etched in my mind. I see them waiting in the morning stillness and catch a word or two.

They soon start to talk and laugh at something or other and get serious when they talk about the weather and then about the war. I remember the patriotic slogan to promote the cause of freedom by sending cigarettes to our fighting men and women overseas. The message is, "Nuts to you and smokes to them!"

Listen! What sort of thunder comes my way? I hear in the brazen air clear-cutting strokes of a whip, and Horwood's horses' hooves come galloping over cobblestones with a devil-may-care alacrity. The driver is behind it all—seated on an old coarse plank attached to a four-wheeled cart.

As soon as the streetcar arrives, passengers get on board and find their seats. I look up at the man in control, the genial, red-faced conductor, Fatty Joy, and he catches my eye. He knows what's on my mind by seeing I am in a ready-set-go stance.

Earlier in the year I remember a middle-aged woman getting on board near Sudbury Street. She was breathing fast and was moaning enough to be heard, "This high step makes it hard to get my body up." Fatty Joy consoled the woman, "I know what you mean, my dear; I'm almost a cartload meself."

The conductor's expression shows his mouth is set in an unyielding line. The streetcar lurches forward, and I am on my way down the strip as fast as my feet can carry me. My strategy is to give nothing less than what is mine to give. Running is happiness. Running is, I bear in mind, a great escape.

I swing myself into a running motion and am a little ahead at Victoria Park where Bridie Cole will soon be organizing sundry games and races. If anyone is an inspiration to sport in St. John's, Bridie is the quintessential one.

I hear the tapping of my footsteps upon the sidewalk. I don't wish to run over the cracks, but to make any changes will throw off my rhythm. I begin to discard that customary habit. I hear, too, the rapid lub-dub-dubbing of the heartbeats against my rib cage loud and clear. I exhale to the fullest extent. I soon follow this by inhaling the majestic air to unlock my heart.

Unfortunately, I am behind at Whittle's Meat Market. It's both funny and strange to see a dead pig in the window with a red rosy apple stuck in its mouth. There is Mr. Whittle, dead serious, and dressed immaculately in white, much like the surgeon prepared to perform the most critical operation.

When I get near Patrick Street, I look up where Wesley United Church stands. This is the place where God plays hide-and-seek with me.

Now I'm having fun as I go ahead of the streetcar at the West End Bazaar. Thank God for all the car stops that enable me to compensate for any digressions along the route. At times I keep track of my nemesis, Fatty Joy, with a secret backward glance, and when he springs ahead, I say to myself, "Hold it! Don't go so fast!"

City sounds fill the air. This is the place where church bells ring. You may hear bells any time at all. Motor cars come and go.

I hear the train as it clicks and clacks its way interminably along, and I hear its whistle as it dissipates itself into the hub of my world. I can hear the grating sounds women make with their high heel shoes as they pick their way carefully over the cobblestone street. The jaded sun appears to compete with the morning chill.

Nothing matters, though, for my sneakers are like similes and my feet are metaphors for life. I must learn to concentrate by getting my second wind. Once in a while Fatty winks at me, and I wave to him.

I usually run on the sidewalk, but every so often I have to run on the street to avoid pedestrians who may get in my way or I in theirs. The streetcar picks up speed, passes me, and rings its bell at the York Theatre. Opposite the York, on my right, is Steers Cove with its flappings, and flutterings, and great bulgings of white sails of schooners. I watch the white seagulls circle and I hear their wailings in the harbor.

I realize I have to run faster. Right now I am about even at the Crescent Theatre. I will be there with my friends in the afternoon for our round of serials. We will jingle our coppers, our sacred coins. We will make our crusade to the Crescent for our visual delights and watch our legion of heroes upon the screen.

As unimportant as it is now, it was vital to me then because I became the victor on Water Street by beating Fatty Joy to Adelaide.

PERSEVERANCE:
GIVE IT EVERYTHING

I remember a young boy, Tom Dempsey, who was disabled at birth. Unfortunately, he was born without a right foot and had only a stub of a right arm.

Yet he dreamed about taking part in sports. He even expressed an ambition to play football. Can you imagine his dream? Because of his positive attitude and grim determination, his parents had an artificial foot made for him.

The foot was made of wood and it was encased in a special stubby football boot. Hour after hour, day after day, month after month, and year after year, Tom Dempsey practiced kicking the football as hard as he could with his wooden foot.

Tom tried and tried to make field goals at greater distances. In time he became so efficient that he was hired by a professional football team—the New Orleans Saints, no less.

Although this event occurred on November 8, 1970, I can still hear the screams of over 65,000 football fans throughout America when, within the last two seconds of the game, Tom, with his crippled foot, kicked a record-breaking 63-yard field goal.

At the time it was the longest field goal ever kicked in a professional football game. As a matter of fact, it gave the Saints a winning score of 19 to 17 over the Detroit Lions.

The Detroit coach, Joe Schmidt, said of Dempsey: "We weren't beaten by a team; we were beaten by a miracle today."

So you see what a man Tom Dempsey was made of, but what does this story mean to you readers out there?

Well, let me tell you there is no such a thing as a handicapped person, no such thing as a problem student, since greatness can come to you when you decide to develop that burning desire within you to achieve your highest goals. The choice is yours and, no matter what you do in life, "Give It All You've Got Because That's What It Takes To Give."

THE BOY WITH
THE SHAKES

There is Tommy Laughlin as poor as poor can be, but if you tell it to his face, he'll look at you as if you have two heads on your shoulders. During the Great Depression, the world was in for a big letdown, generally speaking. In Newfoundland, for instance, the island was left in dire straits. Indeed, the value of the fisheries, the mainstay of the island's economy, had declined close to fifty percent. At least one quarter of its residents were on government relief for such staples as tea, flour, pork, and molasses. Those who were on the dole were receiving six cents a day from the government.

Unfortunately, in the early years of the depression, Mr. Laughlin died from a heart attack unexpectedly. Tommy was only about seven years old at the time. His mother, in the meantime, took in washing to help improve her family's standard of living. As a single mother with seven young children, she never seems to make enough money to pay her bills. Nevertheless, her faith remains unshakeable, and she works hard and never gives up hope.

When Tommy's friend, Fred Powell, comes

out his door chewing on a red rosy apple, Tommy asks him, "Bits on ye?" Fred only says, "Yum" which he believes stands for a yes so far as he knows. Fred is relishing his apple while Tommy looks at him begrudgingly, but bides his time. He stares at his friend as if to say, "When are you going to turn over this apple?" Suddenly, Fred's nose is running down on the fruit and Tommy looks at him in disgust. Finally, Fred passes the stalk to Tommy who is overheard saying, after the fact, "I enjoyed the apple and its taste of brine, when I was ten in '39."

When I was at his house once, I daresay it was in late fall, I noticed the house was very cold at the time. I noticed something else that bothered me, and I inquired of him, "Tommy, how come you have no mirrors in your house?"

"Who needs mirrors? We can do without them. Anyway, we already know what we look like. In our house, we don't need to see in a mirror. All we need do is to see enough to come in the front door and, when the time arrives, go out the back."

Tommy is frail and thin as a rail, and his body shakes from hunger. As a matter of fact, he trembles as well and even his voice has a little quiver. Then, out of the blue, my conscience is in the pulpit, "Look here! If there's someone in want, shouldn't you, if there's a trifle of goodness in your soul, come to the fore and help salve his wounds?"

"Or will you just go on your merry way like a nincompoop, and be content to say the poor we will have with us always and discard it with a solitary amen? What good is it if you're a Christian, and you see a man drowning in a lake. Will you shout out to him, 'Sir, hang on! Don't worry! In the meantime, say a prayer and in a short while I'll be there.'"

Tommy, though, reads his Bible faithfully and tells me some interesting things he learned from his readings.

"You know, George, in the Lord's Prayer there's no mention of me, myself, and I."

"I never noticed that, but you're right, come to think of it."

"So it's not 'my Father,' or 'give me my daily bread,' or 'forgive me my trespasses.'" As a result, I learn that, according to Tommy's message, we don't have to put ourselves first and must try to think of others before we dwell on ourselves. Hmm.

On another day, Tommy and I are going to the Crescent Theatre to see "Tarzan of the Apes." About an hour before we are to leave, my friend comes by and he tells me, "I don't know, George, but I must tell you I'm losing my sole."

"O course, I know you're kidding."

"Yes! I meant it as a joke. Yesterday, though,

93

I was coming home from an errand for my mother, and the sole of my right boot was beginning to fall off. A lot of people were looking at me and, I suppose, wrote me off as a poor angishore (rascal). Some of them stopped and stared at me peculiarly while I kept treading on my sole, for it bunched up as I walked. It was embarrassing for me, but it didn't take long to get used to it. In order to walk normal, I had to sort of flick my foot fast forward so the sole would return flat on the sidewalk. Perhaps I will tie the sole together to the boot and let it go at that."

"What about taking your boot down to the Modern Shoe Hospital on Water Street?"

"I would if I could, but I hear they're mighty dear (costly)."

"But, Tommy, this hospital is exactly the place where they mend sick soles not to talk of boots and shoes."

"There you go—off on a tangent again."

"Yes! You can do that all right. But I have another idea. Come down to my basement and I will save your sole for all time."

"Now you're getting back at me,"

"Isn't that only fair play, Tommy?"

"You're right! I can take a joke as well as the next."

"Let me ask you, do you want your sole to last?"

"Yes, that will be fine."

Tommy watches me in action as I take his boot and cut off the sole because it has too many holes in it anyway. Second, I place a new piece of leather underneath the boot and scribe it out as carefully as I can. Third, I chisel off the extra leather. Fourth, I pick up my father's last and put it on his workbench and take the boot and place it upside down so it fits over the machine. The last thing I have to do is tack the leather to the boot and it's finished.

"There, Tommy Laughlin, there's your shoe almost as good as new. Just remember one thing, if anyone asks about me, tell them I was the one who saved your sole."

"Yeh, right! Good Heavens, I can't believe it. You're wonderful and you've made my day. How come you know how to tap your own boots?"

"My father helps me a lot. To tell the truth, it took me a long time to mend my own soles and put on new heels. I could never have done it without my Dad."

"O my! That's why it must be so wonderful to have a father. I'm sure my father would have helped me, too, if he were only here. God rest his soul."

"When we come back after the serial, if we have time, I will sand down the new piece of leather and polish it so your sole blends in with the rest of your boot."

We are entranced as we follow Tarzan created by that genius, Edgar Rice Burroughs. This is our great escape on a Saturday afternoon for we inherit a high level of mental prowess in Tarzan who stretches our imagination beyond to a place where we wish to be. We follow Tarzan as if he were some kind of idol, some kind of god. We know Tarzan, and we idolize Johnny Weissmuller as if he were one of the greats in our family of heroes. Now I see things in a much better light, that is, once the lackadaisical attitude has been purged from my brain.

We coopy down and play marbles; I play in earnest, but Tommy can care less about winning. All he wishes to do is to play for fun. After the game is finished, I invite him over to my house for a bite to eat.

It's high time I look at some of the intangibles in life that matter in this world of ours if we wish to be happy souls on earth. My mother already knows Tommy has no father and that his mother washes her neighbours' clothes to eke out a living.

As soon as I open the kitchen door, I notice my mother is taking bread out of the oven. "Mom! I'd like you to meet a friend of mine, Tommy Laughlin. Remember I told you about him the other day?"

"Yes! Of course!" She speaks to Tommy in a cordial way, "You're just in the nick of time.

Sit down here at the kitchen table and let's have some tea."

He replies, "Thank you, Mrs. Hillier, for having me. 'Tis a lovely day, isn't it?"

"Don't mention it, my boy! Glad to have you. Yes, it is a lovely day. At least, it sure beats all the rain, drizzle, and fog we've had lately."

From the corner of my eye, I can see his eyes flitting about: on the ceiling, on the bright mint green painted walls of the kitchen and, as he sees our stove, his face is beaming,

"My heavens, what a snazzy stove!"

"You know, Tommy, my father picked out this stove we bought at the United Nail Foundry. It's called the UNF Special. I feel almost as good as you do about it. My mother's brother who is my uncle, Peter Rockwood, works at the foundry, and fixed the stove in place for us three weeks ago. What's more, and this is truly amazing, it was manufactured by an angel."

"Gwan with ye, George! You're just joshing me."

"Truth to tell, it was an angel, but a Frederick W. Angel, B.Sc., A.M.E.I.C., and M.B.E. He lives on 146 Hamilton Avenue. I pass his house every day on the way to Centenary Hall School and three times on Sunday on the way to Wesley United Church on Patrick Street."

"Son," my mother says, "I think that's enough

for now. Another time, you can talk about being at the foundry and telling us how exciting it was when you told me about the white-hot molten iron filling up the molds. My son thinks the Angels are geniuses, anyway."

"Sorry, Tommy! I got carried away."

"That's all right. It's got to happen to all of us someday."

My mother slices the bread, butters it, and brings out the marmalade. Tommy's face lights up as if the sun is shining on his countenance. As I survey our guest, I've never seen his face as brilliant as it is today. Between bites, he manages to say, "Thank you, missus, for your kindness. If the rights were known, I do believe you're sp'ilin' me. Isn't that so, George?"

"Yes, but in this case, a little sp'ilin' will do you the world of good. You deserve this sort of treatment. I know for sure my mother and I are pleased to have you as company—as if you're a brother or my mother's son."

"May I say something?"

"By all means, my boy," says my mother.

"Missus, how many children do you have?"

"Seven in all."

"Well, then, you already have enough to do without fussing over me."

"Really, Tommy, it's no bother and it's no fuss."

"I want you to know this has got to be the

loveliest time I've ever had since I don't know when."

My mother speaks, "You are always welcome in our house anytime. Don't be a stranger."

Several days later, Tommy Laughlin comes to our house with a most ingratiating smile on his face. As my mother opens the door, he tells her,

"I want you to know, Mrs. Hillier, the partridge berries in this bowl are for you and your family. I picked them for you on the Southside Hills this very morning."

"You mean to say you walked way up to those hills just to pick berries? Why on earth would you want to pick berries on such a wet, drizzly day? If you don't watch out, you're going to catch your death of cold."

"The rain doesn't bother me at all. When it rains, it just means your partridge berries are so much the fresher and, maybe, even sweeter."

My mother comes down from the porch, holds Tommy in her arms, and kisses him on the cheek. For all that and all that, Tommy goes on with his life and never complains. Evidently, he's a young boy with the patience of Job. As I look at him, I begin to praise him in my mind because he is the sort of guy who goes out of his way to find such good in life such as it is. If the fog is as thick as pea soup, he will tell you, "Don't fret! The sun will come out yet; just you wait and see."

In the fall, Tommy and his older brother, Dermot, came by our house with a brace of rabbits and handed them to my mother who was overjoyed with such a pleasant surprise, "I want to pay you for these rabbits!"

"No way, missus! I won't talk of it. They're yours!" says Tommy. "Dermot and I snared them early this morning."

I have saved some money from my paper route, and on another day, I ask Tommy, "How would you like to come down with me to New Gower Street for a feed of Stacey's Fish & Chips?"

"Are you kidding me?"

"No! Of course not!"

"Do you like fish and chips?"

"Yes! Yes! Especially Stacey's. Put it to the test: Stacey's Fish & Chips are better than the best."

As we walk down Water Street, I can't believe it when I see Tommy walking nonchalantly on the cracks of the sidewalk. I avoid them like the plague. So I question him, "You don't seem to mind walking on the cracks, just like that?"

"Of course not! I'm not that silly or superstitious about things. I have more things on my mind than to worry about the daffy things in life."

When we get to Stacey's, I introduce my guest to my Uncle Jim Stacey who looks handsome and so resplendent in his immaculate white apron. He takes us over to a table near a window. My uncle is most obliging, and over the years he has treated me many times to his delicious fish and chips. This time, however, I can pay my own way. I find it interesting to note that Tommy doesn't seem to be shaking anymore.

Perhaps, it's the result of the scrumptious aroma that's coming from the kitchen. Or the heavenly omen to suggest that relief is on the way. When I look at Tommy, the choir boy from St. Patrick's Church, with his worn-out salt and pepper sweater on, I know about the poor and needy, and I remind myself that I have to feel fortunate and must thank my lucky stars.

Now words come instantly to mind, those same words which I keep to myself, "Did not I weep for him that was in trouble? Was not my soul grieved for the poor?" (Job 30:10) My Uncle Jim puts everything before us. I am ecstatic and Tommy is most appreciative and says, "George, you shouldn't have done that for me, above all people."

"Tommy, are you pleased you came here?"

"Yes, by all means for a boy with no means."

"OK then! Let's dig in!"

"Just a minute, George!"

"Why, what's wrong?"

"You must know flat out I've never had such a meal as this in all my born days. I'm so happy

I could cry." He doesn't cry, but the tears run down his cheeks automatically, and he wipes them away with a corner of his sleeve.

"Remember, you don't have to cry for your supper like Tommy Tucker. You're here to be happy—not sad."

"No, George! I have to say a little grace. This is a special treat for me, and I don't want it to go unnoticed."

"Ok, Tommy! Who's hungry, you or me?"

Tommy proceeds with grace,

> You cannot pray the Lord's prayer,
> and even once say "I."
> You cannot pray the Lord's prayer,
> And even once say "My."
> Nor can you pray the Lord's prayer,
> And not pray for another;
> For when you ask for daily bread,
> You must include your brother.
> For others are included
> In each and every plea:
> From the beginning to the end of it,
> It does not once say "Me."
> Amen

"Thanks, Tommy! It's most gracious of you. Pray tell, where did you get that kind of grace?"

Tommy looks over and winks at me and says,

"That's for me to know and you to find out."

When I look back over the years, although I haven't seen Tommy after I went away, I think of his becoming a man, an integral part of all men, as good as most men, and in the final analysis, far better a man than many. I care about humanity, and I consider the evil in the world with people massing together superfluous riches without any regard for the welfare of others.

It is then I conclude that Tommy Laughlin was not merely a rich man or a poor man. In my estimation, he was the essence of a noble man whose kind will be sorely missed upon this blessed earth.

WHEN RIGHTEOUSNESS GETS LOST ON EARTH

To make a better world makes better sense,
But nations make a mockery of peace
For there's no honor system, just pretense
While hist'ry tells us wars may never cease.
We rise above the laughter and the tears
So that a common trust becomes our goal,
But shocks of sudden change pronounce
    stark fears
And reign within the virtue of the soul.
The urge to strike first or retaliate?
Proud forces break upon a fragile land
In times of crisis, time to escalate
As ashes empty into burning sand.
Those fears remain and logic soon departs
When righteousness is lost in human hearts.

"EVERY DAY DOING . . . THE VERY BEST I CAN."

MAX MERCER — A TRIBUTE

I just heard the news about Max Mercer's death today. It was indeed my pleasure to have met with him several times in early August. Although by no means a keen observer of mankind, I would like, nonetheless, to express some of my emotions and sentiments about the species of this man.

I hadn't seen Max for over twenty years, but always remembered him as an excellent photographer, a decent artist, and in later years, as an accomplished businessman. I remember him too as a true Newfoundlander who loved his country and was sincerely interested in its future.

Most importantly, however, I remember his constant smile. He seemed so happy about life and was always ready to make you laugh about something or other, ready or not, so you could share in this happiness.

His philosophy of life was downright positive and very impressive right up to the end. Perhaps we may all be able to learn some kind of lesson from it.

While he was in the hospital, taking his giant

step toward recovery, showing no signs of self-pity or bitterness, Max cherished his conviction about setting up a handicrafts center at home. He had a passionate love for all of his projects that helped to add so much enthusiasm and such strength to his life.

Out of curiosity or just as an innovation, he was always ready to initiate any venture that appealed to him.

Often irritable or impatient unless he was doing something, as usually he was, he said to me just recently, "Every day, come hell or high water, I am going to go on doing the very best I can. I am interested in life—not in its alternative."

With courage blazing forth like the noon day sun, he convinced me that the world could be mastered from within the confines of four posts of a bed.

What was the feeling like, to go on living, enduring intolerable pain, becoming blind, losing a leg, and then having to undergo a kidney transplant, all as an aftermath of diabetes? I don't have the answer to that question right now, but surely Max did.

It is difficult to know about the workings of the mind, but it seemed to me that the zest for living still brewed in his head. He talked logically and most enthusiastically about life, and like a brave soldier was prepared in every way to fight for it.

He shared his optimism with his wife Susan, with his friends, and with the hospital staff that cared so much for him. Hope would spring either from a good day or from any promising report he could get about his health. Life could still be enjoyed, even when conditioned by all the pain.

In the noblest sense this man fought on most courageously—he didn't want to give up. He never surrendered at all. If any person is to be judged by virtues, it is said that "courage" just like cream, in essence, will always manage to rise up to the top.

It may concern us to think that while some people may talk idly about life, sit still and ponder over it, Max had already lived life, was enriched by it, and had enjoyed every last minute of it.

If we could ourselves summon up such courage and vision for our own lives, by bucking the tough obstacles and disappointments, then perhaps, there could be no way by which we could be defeated by life.

Max was not able to finish all of his plans and dreams, but he demonstrated that he had the ability and the guts to do so.

After all, is it reaching the goals in life that really count, or is it the lessons we meet along the way that really matter?

I'm not sorry in any way for this man, instead

I am sorry for mankind whose future course may be judged more by despair than by hope, more by hate than by love, and more by frustration than by fulfillment.

Max wanted to change all that; perhaps from his fine example, we may want to improve some of the ways in our own lives. His life and the courage in which he lived it may now become our reward. By his example, he has offered us a penny for our thoughts. That penny, inestimable in value, may some day be worth a fortune to us.

This man was the Max I remember.

He was a man I shall never forget.

A NEW PAIR OF SNEAKERS

Ideas are cut from the fabric of yesterday's memories. I remember my mother going downtown on a Friday afternoon of March, 1940, to buy me a brand new pair of sneakers at Parker & Monroe. I am thrilled for my mere self. For a shy 10-year-old, it is like getting a Christmas present.

When my mother put the sneakers in my arms, I projected my nose inside them, just to smell the quality of their freshness. I shall never forget that experience because I have some idea how much my mother had to stretch the dollars my father earned as a carpenter at Horwood Lumber Company.

When I was a 12-year old *Telegram* newsboy, I became enamored of running by watching the surreal scene of Pat Kelly, straining at the bit, while running along Duckworth Street toward the finish line and capturing *The Evening Telegram* 10-Mile Road Race in the city. Indeed, Pat was an awesome sight with his powerful physique along with his winning smile.

At that moment, I knew for sure that I wanted to run this race and do my level best to emulate Pat Kelly who was my hero to behold. I bided my time and when I was seventeen, I decided to practice by running in order to follow in my hero's footsteps. After training for one month, I felt I was ready to do a test run at the Feildian Grounds east of the city.

Since I was quite shy at the time, I waited until it got dark, and then I stepped on the one-quarter mile track. I realized it would take 40 laps around the track to find out what my time would be. When I finished, I checked my stopwatch. Unfortunately, my time was most disappointing since it took me 67 minutes and 53 seconds to complete ten miles.

Most of the winners would usually finish inside of 60 minutes. At least, I did finish, yet I realize that my time would never put me in first place. Nevertheless, I stayed the course and performed admirably by winning the ten-mile race in 1950 with a time of 55 minutes and 40 seconds.

I remember once asking my father how far it is to his work. He is leaning up against a wall near the kitchen door. He rolls his cigarette, seals it, and then thinks about my question for a moment. "Hmm. Let me see. One . . . two . . . three . . . four . . . five . . . six! That's it!"

"Six miles?" I ask.

"O, no, my son! Six cigarettes! Three to get me there and three to bring me home."

My mother was a fussy housekeeper. She gave me a tongue-banging one day for having left my sweaty socks on my bedroom floor. I can hear her call out to me, "My heavens, George, what ails you? Put your socks down in the basement; we're having company tonight!"

The next morning, Saturday, I get up, take my sponge bath, and make sure my body is scrupulously clean. I get into my long underwear, Stanfield's Excelsior, shake powder inside my white woolen socks, and then don my green corduroy breeks with their patched knees.

In fact, my mother sewed patches upon patches of patches that were already there so my sacred breeks would last forever. I wear a hand-made khaki shirt, put braces over my shirt, pull my socks up just below the knees; lastly, I lace up my sneakers good and tight.

When I go downstairs I eat my rolled oats and molasses mix, drink a cup of tea, have toast and marmalade, and finish everything off with two heaping tablespoonfuls of pure cod liver oil to make up for the sun's loss and to keep the colds away.

Not long after breakfast, I tell my mother, "Mom! I'm going to race the streetcar today." She looks at me a bit surprised, "What next? Well, I never! Whatever you do, be careful. Watch out for the traffic! O, do you have clean underwear on?"

"Yes!"

With my black mittens, a brown suede jacket,

a black skull cap, and a swagger stick in my right hand, I am ready to face the day. My mother sits on a rocking chair and begins to knit a sweater.

I'm amazed at her actions. Her fingers move incredibly fast with her knit-one purl-two effect while the needles carry their clicking, rhythmical sounds.

When I come out the door, Mr. Jeremiah Farrell, our next-door neighbor, is already outside as he talks to passers-by in his rich brogue, with his ready-to-spin yarns and honest-to-goodness exaggerations.

Mr. Farrell is an avid reader who reads everything in sight and, as a result, is never lost for words. He is heavy on humor. Here is one of his characteristic treats:

"There was an old lady from Sligo
Who went where all those who die go.
When she got to the gate,
She says, 'I'm only 28!'
And now she goes where all those who lie go."

Jeremiah is no ordinary man. He is cast in an heroic mould, a survivor, albeit with his left leg missing, having been struck-off-the strength at Beaumont Hamel. Few members of the Newfoundland Regiment survived. Jeremiah is one of them.

Mr. Farrell is a true Newfoundlander, but his complexion changes, however, when it comes to Saint Patrick's Day. Then he turns Irish, wags his long white beard up and down, and exults with boyish delight, "This is the day when my green, green ribbon will twist the bloody tail of the English lion!" I swear he is a survivor because he knows how to lay bare the soul of his wit.

The unruly easterly bends the chimney smoke of the houses on McKay Street on days when happiness is a bin full of Morey's coal. This is the street where all sorts of games and sports are played: horseshoes, hopscotch, marbles, tag, football (soccer), hockey, jacks, hoist-your-sails and run, softball and running around the block. Running is the sport to provide me with an outlet.

IF YOU SHOULD EVER ASK ME, "WHAT IS FALL?"

Fall flies fast, circles out, and disappears
after its deep, imprisoned melody.
We have kaleidoscopes to name our own
coloring. It is the time for telling
someone we're haunted by a ghost. Fall puts
us on hold, implores us to make chaos
yield to order. Fall is hideous, bare,
hungry, weary, panting, and recumbent,
immobile and supine. If we listen
we hear its echoes in a hollow bell,
ringing. Soon we hear its fingers snapping.
What violence for the ears. Fall is wrinkled,
thin and haggard. Its superstitious eyes
whirl round and round furiously. Yet Fall
tells us something about its history
in breathless hurry. What a specimen
it is for bloodshot eyes. O, how we lose
our self-possession to a moment's thought.
Fall, though, speaks much more elegantly than
the mind and remains beautiful. What are
our thoughts? We have them. Fall sinks slowly,
silently, down, down, down, without pausing.
There is no sound sometimes. How swarthy and
how sinister. It breaks up our sleep. Yet,

look how it is benevolently bent.
It frames itself against conspiracy,
But what is Fall? Of course, we're standing
here,
smiling, staring hard at the pictures. Persist.

THE GREAT BLIZZARD OF '78 IN BOSTON, MA

Full-throated flourish, restless in its sweep,
A mere snowflake in multitudes of flight,
Sparkles, sprinkles in blinding record set,
Soon strangles everything within its sight.

The storm scatters to rough smooth
    features out,
Knocks and quickens the pulse of everyone
On such a cold and frosty winter's day,
Like the hard lashing from a mother's tongue.

Twisted, imprisoned, entangled people
In this God-forsaken place, no-man's land,
Abandon cars in nature's bedlam flight
As shore walls fall to raging seas and wind.

So tough to warm the wind that winter blows
Upon windows hearing the awesome beat;
The storm, so fast and furious, picks up,
Staggers the mind and rocks us off our feet.

Angry seas swallow Peter Stuyvesant,
Lost is the art of Motif Number One;
Many homeless, lose everything they had
And too many who fought are gone, are gone.

There is hope in time to overcome fears:
Those in love with courageous sentiments,
Saying very little, but doing much,
Embattled, they battled the elements.

Triumphant now to face much tougher times,
Preparing for whatever life will bring,
New Englanders know how to take a stand,
Lying in wait to hear the voice of Spring.

WILL WINTER QUESTIONS HAVE REPLIES BY SPRING?

Time is the bell that strikes with measured
   blows
While we are always conjuring up peace.
My bones are set for coldest winter snows
But passion spent on wars shall never cease.
The heart resumes its task on getting old
Yet love will wreak from life its offering.
Though snow keeps falling and the wind
   is cold:
Will winter questions have replies by spring?
Our lives hold on to ease the loneliness
But soon the leaves and branches break away
In this wide world wild in its wilderness
Gives life its moments on a summer's day.
We know the time that days are measured on
And do not ask where have the years all gone.

THE COLLEEN FROM KINSALE

Josie Fitzgerald is the aunt to the Mahon family: John, Jimmy, Ann, Dick, Tommy, and Joan. They are all married now, and they live in Massachusetts except for Joan who lives in Rhode Island. Josie is the proverbial worthy advisor to all their families.

I meet with Josie in her retirement home in Drake Village in Arlington, Massachusetts. If I remember rightly, it was in the winter of 1986. She tells me she was born Johanna Whyte in Castle Park, Kinsale, in County Cork, Ireland, on June 6, 1901. "That was the exact time when my mother had a conniption," so she tells me. I take one look at her and realize she is kidding me.

"You know," she says, "they took out the 'y' in our name and put in an 'i' instead. I'm not sure why that was done. Maybe it made the name easier to spell, or else it became more commonplace. Anyway, I'm certain hardly anyone would ever spell out our name: 'W-h-y-t-e.' "

"Now let's have tea. Also for this special occasion, I baked scones for you as a treat.

The recipe comes across the sea from Kinsale, Ireland, I have ye know."

"Thank you, Josie. You shouldn't have gone to all that trouble for me."

"Why not? You're deserving as much as the others."

"You know it must not have been easy leaving your home in Kinsale."

" 'Twas mighty hard breaking away. I suppose the saddest thing was to say goodbye to my parents after being with them on the farm all those years. The sensations at that moment were too painfully vivid to ever be forgotten. When I kissed my mother, I held her in my arms, and we both had a good cry. She says to me, 'Here, take this money I put aside for your going. I'm glad you'll be with your sister (Catherine) again. I have ye know, her husband, John, is a very fine man.' "

"I bet your father hated to see you go, for I remember how you helped him on the farm so much."

"My father wasn't thrilled about my leaving, but he came around when he realized I was so anxious to go. His last words to me were, 'Johanna, if you work in America like you worked on the farm, you will be a great success. May God go with ye. And don't forget, Johanna, be strong and of good courage.' "

"Were there any more farewells?"

"O, yes! I said goodbye to my brother, Jimmy, and my sister, Elizabeth, and told them both, 'If you ever decide to come to America yourselves, let me know. I will write to you and tell you how things are after I get settled in.'

"Then I met my boyfriend, Danny Whelan, and we hugged and kissed. I told him, 'Danny, I will tell you how I'm getting on in America, and if I don't like it there, I will come back to you.'"

"Johanna, I hate to see ye go away. I'm not sure what I'm going to do after you're gone. Please take good care of yourself. Now I have an Irish blessing I'd like to read to you. It goes this way:

'May God in his wisdom
And infinite love
Look down on you always
From Heaven above.
May he send you good fortune,
Contentment and peace
And may all your blessings
Forever increase.'"

"O, my! Danny, that sounds beautiful. Is that your poem?"

"Not likely! I found it in a book, and I kept it just for your leaving."

"Goodbye, Danny. I will be writing to you as soon as I'm able."

• • •

"Josie, before I forget, I must tell you how nice you've been to Janemarie and me over the years. Every time the Mahons had a gathering of the clan, we used to have so much fun whenever we got together. When I came over to your table, I'd never forget to have my pencil and notepad ready, because I learn from you the same way I learn from others. Now I can understand why you were the best in class when it came to history. Indeed, you were never lost for words, especially when it came to Irish history. You know, I've kept all the notes about the information I received from you over the years."

"I thank you and your dear wife. I know for sure, the lovely thing married beneath her." Josie and I would make jokes about one another with no malice of forethought.

"Of course, we had grand times at our Christmas parties. There was always something or other going on to celebrate a cause."

"Josie, on behalf of the Mahon families, I must say sincerely, you've been the soul of generosity to all of them: John, Jimmy, Ann, Dick, Tommy, and Joan."

"In all seriousness, George, we must remember who started it all. So we salute the founding mother, Catherine, and founding father, John, who made our lives so worthwhile. Neither can we dare forget the married couples: John and

Ruth, Jimmy and Ann, Ann and Frank Powers, Dick and Maryanne, Tommy and Gail, and Joan and Mike Barry."

"And doesn't the beat go on, too, Josie? I remember how much you helped all the children and grandchildren whose names and numbers are legion."

"Glory be, yes! I must say I left Ireland because my sister, Catherine, used to write to me about coming to America, and her husband, John, was most welcoming in every way. I say now that God taught me how to face my problems while Catherine and John became my guiding light."

"I know, Josie, how giving you are of your time and effort to make everyone you meet feel so happy about life."

"I'm not alone. What I do is nothing unusual. Mind you, I'm not here to blow my own horn, so to speak, but what I do is motivated by what God tells me to do. I would like the whole wide world to become one big happy family. I follow the Bible closely each day, and when I open the refrigerator, I have a little message on the door with a quote from 2 Corinthians (9:7):

'Every woman according as she proposes in her heart, so let her give, not grudgingly, for God loves a cheerful giver.'

"So, George, let me say it clearly: I am a Christian and I still consider myself a sinner in the world. Yet I'm some pleased whenever I do a good deed; I look into my heart, and believe I've climbed one step higher. At any rate, we can all become grateful for the beauty of each day and to help God spread the love that surrounds us all."

"What's this on the wall there? It sure looks like a Psalm."

"Indeed it is a Psalm and it's the 67th. This is in my own handwriting."

"It's beautiful script."

"I brought it over with me from Ireland. I grew up with this Psalm that tells us about God spreading His kingdom on earth. I don't recall the entire Psalm except for these verses:

'May God be gracious to us and bless us and make His face to shine upon us that your way may be known upon earth, your saving power among all nations. Let the people praise You, O God; let all the people praise You.' "

As I sit in Josie's living room, I see a large painting on the wall before me. "I see a beautiful painting. What an idyllic scene this is."

"This is Kinsale, the place where I was born until I left in '21. When we finish eating, I will tell you more about the village's major points of interest. In the meantime, promise me that you and Janemarie will visit Kinsale, that is, if you are able some year."

"As God is my judge, Janemarie and I will

take a trip if not this year, then next year. That's not just a promise—'tis guaranteed!"

"Just a minute. I have to get a pointer to show you what's going on.

"To the left there is St. Multose Church that was built in the 12th century. I've attended many religious services there. Truth to tell, a man by the name of Multose started a monastery here around the 6th century, and the town of Kinsale grew up around St. Multose. It was constructed by the Normans around 1190 on top of the remains of the old monastery. If you must know, St. Multose is the patron saint of Kinsale, and his Feast Day is on December 11th.

"Right here is about where the courthouse stands. It is now Kinsale's Regional Museum. It's interesting for you to know that there's a display about the sums that were raised on goods coming through the town gates. There's one exception to a levy that states, 'No fee is to be taken out of a smaller quantity of potatoes than three weights brought to town on women's or children's backs.'

"Here is Compass Hill and when you go there, you will see the remains of houses built in the style of its occupants: The French, Spanish, and English."

"Might that be a good place to stay when we're over there?"

"Indeed! I'm some glad you mentioned it. This is a grand place to rent. There's a big sitting room and a bay window from which you can get an excellent view of the village and the harbor, its river, and the houses nearby. There's also an open fire and a lovely kitchen and a garden along with a patio to the rear."

"What about a place to eat? I hear that Kinsale is the Food Center in Ireland. After all, we got to eat sometime, Josie."

"Begor! What a comic you're letting on to be. Worry not! Compass Hill has gourmet restaurants all around you. And what's more, the finest food you can ever wish to eat."

"Now let me explain a few more things. Here you see a tip of land: this is the Old Head of Kinsale. Right here is the site where Norman DeCourcy built his castle in the 16th century over an old stone fort which was the thing to do in those days. It must have been sold; I believe it is called the Desmond Castle now."

"Do ye see where I'm pointing, George?"

"I got you, Josie. I'm impressed with your knowledge. In fact, if I could, I'd jump at the chance to go right there this instant. You paint a glorious picture of Kinsale."

"Look out there! Not too far beyond the cliffs is where the Lusitania was torpedoed on 7th May, 1915. Unfortunately, the Kinsale fishermen got to their boats to rescue the passengers, but the English warning was that they were not allowed to go there. That came as a commandment to the Irish."

"A total of 1,198 people drowned on that day when a German submarine sunk the Lusitania that rolled over and sank in 18 minutes. I'm sure that the fishermen could have saved many lives if they had been given the opportunity to do so."

"I can't believe the English were so bloody hard-hearted. Many lives could have been rescued on that day. That's uncanny! That's absurd!"

"Remember, George, we were under English rule. Our hands were tied, so to speak. I must tell you, not all Protestants in Ireland were in sympathy with English rule. I'm giving you a letter from a Protestant minister who represents many views in support of the Irish cause."

I read the letter Josie gave me and decided to put it into print to let everyone know about the plight of the Irish:

"To Isaac Butt, Esq. L.L.D.

My Dear Butt,

If every other man in the world entertained doubts of my sincerity, you, at least, would give me credit for honesty and just intentions. I write to you accordingly, because my mind has been stirred to its inmost depths by the perusal of your address in my native city of Limerick. I do not regard the subject of your address as a political one. It ought to be regarded solely as a question of humanity, justice, common sense, and common honesty. I wish my lot had never been cast in rural places. As a clergyman, I hear what neither landlords nor agents ever heard. I see the depression of the people; their sighs and groans are before me. They are brought so low as often to praise and glorify those whom, in their secret hearts, are the objects of abhorrence. All this came out gradually before me. Nor did I feel as I ought to have felt in their behalf, until, in my own person and purse, I became the victim of a system of tyranny which cries from earth to heaven for relief. Were I to narrate my own story, it would startle many of the Protestants of Ireland. There are good landlords—never a better than the late Lord Downshire, or the living and beloved Lord Roden. But there are too many of another state of feeling and action. There are estates in the north where the screw is never withdrawn from its circuitous and oppressive work. Tenant-right is an unfortunate and delusive affair, simply because it is invariably used to the landlord's advantage. Here we have an election in prospect, and in many counties no farmer will be permitted to think or act for himself. What right any one man has to demand the surrender of another's vote I never could see. It is an act of sheer felony—a perfect "stand-and-deliver" affair. To hear a man slavishly and timorously say, 'I must give my vote as the landlord wishes,' is an admission that the Legislature, which bestowed the right of voting on the tenant, should not see him robbed of his right, or subsequently scourged or banished from house and land, because he disregarded a landlord's nod, or the menace of a land-agent. At no little hazard of losing the friendship of some who are high, and good, and kind, I write this as I do.

Yours my dear Butt, very sincerely,
Thomas Drew

Dundrum, Clough, County Down,
Sept. 7, 1868"

I catch Josie in a talkative, festive mood, "You know my father's father was a Baptist from Wales, but since we were already good Catholics, my father, poor soul, never thought it important enough to remind us we once had sprung from Baptist roots."

When Josie was a pupil at the Ring Rone School in Kinsale, she had very high marks in all her subjects. Evidently, she worked like a Trojan, loved school, and was even hoping to be a teacher some day.

She tells me that the pupils in Ireland were not permitted to read any material related to America. So when the supervisor came to evaluate the schools, the teachers would hide the American texts in the cupboards until he left the premises. Also, the schools were denominational, and she tells me, "The Catholics and Protestants attended different schools, but once in awhile, we had some Protestant pupils since they lived close by. They usually left before catechism time. We'd poke fun at our parochial ways, and in the playgrounds you can hear such rhymes as:

"Red, white, and blue
Should be torn up in two,
And sent to the Devil
At half-past two."

"Up the long ladder,
Down the short rope,
To hell with King Billy,
And God bless the Pope."

"I was always in love with Ireland and its mysteries. Even to this very day, I have not changed one iota."

Josie tells me about the site of a battle in 1601 between the combined forces of Spanish and Irish against the English army.

The English won this battle, and the Gaelic chieftains suffered a most humiliating defeat. This led to what is called "The Flight of the Earls," when many of the Irish aristocrats were compelled to leave their lands and escape to Europe. This defeat in Kinsale marked the end of the Gaelic order in Ireland forever.

An Irish writer, Monie Begley, made reference to "The Flight of the Earls" in 1607, and felt downhearted about the demise of the Irish culture. A poet, Egan O'Rahilly, is embittered by the loss of the Celtic traditions and directs his insults at the kings, the O'Neill and O'Donnell line. He includes them in his lamentation,

"My heart is withered and my health is gone,
For they who were not easy put upon,
Masters of mirth and fair clemency,
Masters of wealth and gentle charity,
They are all gone, Mac Caura Mor is dead,
Mac Caura of Lee is finished,
Mac Caura of Kantuck joined clay to clay
And gat him gone, and bides as deep as they.
Ease thee, cease thy long keening, cry no
        more:
End is, and here is end, and end is sore,
And to all lamentation be there end:

If I might come on thee, O howling friend:
Knowing that sails were drumming on the sea
Westward to Eire, and that help would be
Tramping for her upon a Spanish deck,
I ram thy lamentation down thy neck."

The Whytes were always kept busy with their cows, horses, sheep, and pigs. They grew mainly carrots, cabbage, turnips, beets, and, of course, potatoes. Yet Josie had her dreams and was overwhelmed by wanderlust. She made it known to me, "If I had stayed on the farm, then I was afraid my dreams would have lost most of their reality."

Johanna has been going steady with Danny Whelan and he doesn't want to lose her. "You know, Johanna, we've been courting now for over a year. Don't you think it's high time we got married instead of hangin' on like this?"

"Danny, just look at yourself and now look at me! Who in their right mind would ever want to marry the likes of us?"

"My God, what ails ye, Johanna? What are ye after saying to me?"

"Danny! Danny! It's just a joke. I thought it up for fun. Don't you get it?"

"O, sure! Pshaw! It's very funny. I can't wait to laugh."

"For that matter, I appreciate your feelings, Danny. Don't get me wrong. Let me ask you, what do ye want to do with your life in case we get married?"

"I expect to be a farmer like my father before me. What's so wrong with that, Johanna?"

"That's fine for you, but I've been a farmer's daughter for many years. Somehow I have a hard time believing I'm going to be a farmer's wife. Truth to tell, Danny, I'm not too thrilled with its promises and all."

"But what about tonight? Will ye still go to the dance with me?"

"Of course, Danny! Of course! You may go home now and bless your little heart and every other Irish part."

Finally, Josie left Ireland on May 3, 1925, when she was twenty-three years old. Indubitably, she was filled with hope for a better or, at least, a different way of life. At that time Ireland was still in the throes of a civil war and was experiencing hard times to say the least; there was no human stance as important as the critical demand to be thrifty.

Ever present is the character of relations between landlord and tenant. As a landlord, England's policy was to make money and the natural effect of famine, eviction, and emigration over the years crystallized in the Irish their deep core of animosity toward England and the English.

I hear Josie say, "The Irish Question is always

the question of the day. I daresay the question in my estimation is: 'how can we avenge ourselves and put an end to our suffering here in Ireland?' The Normans conquered the land in Ireland, but the English want us to wither away completely."

The past, though, is deep, sometimes much too deep to touch. As my Great-grandfather, Peter Cassidy, used to say about the past, "It is much too serious a matter to be settled by the use of trivial gloryings."

As soon as Josie arrived in Boston, Massachusetts, she was helped along by her older sister, Catherine, and her husband, John. Soon after, she went to work as a nanny for several years until she received a more enviable position as a clerk at Massachusetts Institute of Technology (MIT). Josie stayed there for twenty-nine years.

Then, in 1944, she married, rather late in life, to a Robert Fitzgerald who used to be a captain in the IRA (Irish Republican Army). Once he became an American citizen, he immediately joined the U.S. army. Together they lived happily on Bow Street in Cambridge, Massachusetts. Unfortunately, Robert died unexpectedly on November 1, 1956. According to Josie, that was "All Saints Day."

I am reminded by one of Josie's relatives that there was another side to her other than the serious side. This was the fun-loving-singing-dancing-laughing side of this colleen's nature. "Begorra," I'm told: "the crack was mighty when Josie was around."

An old friend, Kitty Fogarty, said one time, "O, Josie you were some flirt with the boys when you were young."

Immediately, Josie countered, "Kitty, watch your tongue and mind your manners!" Aw, but, at times, it was said that Josie was so popular with the Irish lads that she had a boy for every single hair on her auburn head.

"I was never so lucky in all my life when I came to America. I am so thankful for everything." Josie Fitzgerald has been retired for many years and is most appreciative of the kindness she has received from M.I.T. in Cambridge, Massachusetts.

"I have to tell you, George, they gave me two pensions when I left there. First, was the regular pension; second, was another pension for never having missed one day in twenty-nine years of working there." I can imagine that this lovely colleen was once a prodigious worker who took so much pride in a job well done.

Josie currently lives at Drake Village where life is rather pleasant, but where it can be both strange and lonely, when she sees so many people come and go. "I see so many people limp and lame. I see them day in and day out. It is then I take one look at myself with only my mere touch of arthritis.

"Yes, I once had a bout with arthritis. 'Twas awful until I had injections in both arms. I swear those gold shots cured me. Even Dr. Dowd reassured me, 'Josie, you are the luckiest woman in Arlington. The gold mixed with your blood perfectly.' "

"Josie," I say, "Since the arthritis disappeared, this could be a miracle for all that. That's what I would call it—a miracle."

"O, George, I don't rightly know. I'm not going to argue with you this time."

With some tears in her eyes and some traces of emotion, Josie's voice weakens a little as soon as she tells me she is the only one alive in her family: "All members of my family have passed away: my mother and father, Catherine, Jimmy, and Elizabeth."

As she indulges in a few exclamations, she wishes to say something, simply and unaffectedly, that she, too, may find herself in Heaven. A wise woman learns to expect some gratitude, after all is said and done, since Heaven is far too delicate a flower for the winds of this earth.

In the meantime, there is a distinct sense of nostalgia in her voice, and the classic emotion in her eyes, indicating she would like to take a sentimental journey back as it were to Ireland, or "Eire," or if you're poetical at all, to "Erin," or what's more, if you're the "compleat" scholar, it's back to "Hibernia." Then, especially, if you're Gaelic, it's "Fohler."

Her memories take her back, back to her home, back to the farm, back to the fields she used to plough, back to the fresh swirling Bandon River, back to the time when her father says to his son, "Jimmy, me b'y, you're going to get somewhere some day just as sure as God put worms in sour apples," back to the fair where Johanna first sold four of her family's cows and five of their pigs, back when she sang "Danny Boy" at a pub, unbeknownst to her father, who would have half-killed her just for being there.

Aw, yes! It's always back when one has gone away for so long a time, back to the grand farms where sad men, broken on the wheel of labor, were too tired and too nerve-worn to look up at the stars.

Josie's memories return on her birthdays, and on St. Patrick's Day, when she still hears the ancient tellers of the fascinating Irish tales. Everything comes back to Johanna, back at last, when angels, whose cheeks were painted red like ripe apples all the time, were busy with their singing and dancing.

O, she remembers Danny Whelan, the red-headed boy with the crooked smile and freckled face, clad in the cast-off clothing of more fortunate relatives. Aw! 'tis true, for as she knows, does Johanna, that the journey only lasts so long. I come to ask my friend of many years, "Josie, how do you know you will go to Heaven?"

"I know," but she still retains her sense of humor and has that certain glimmer in her eye as she smiles at me.

"I absolutely know for sure since I've already made my reservations there."

MOLLY: THE CAIRN TERRIER

The Cairn terrier had its origin over 200 years ago in the Highlands of Scotland as well as on the Isle of Skye. Unfortunately, the history of this breed is rather skimpy in terms of discovering its precise origin. Nevertheless, the Cairn remains one of the oldest pure British terrier breeds. It is a recognizable fact that in the 16th century historians declared the Cairn terriers to be hailed as "The Earth Dogs" from Argyllshire.

It was during the reign of King James VI of Scotland when the king sent six of those earth dogs to some of his friends in France. In the early years, Cairn terriers were useful in hunting foxes and badgers that were hiding habitually in rocky crevices or cairns; hence the term "Cairn" came into being.

My son, George, and his wife, Crisann, have a Cairn terrier named Molly. For the past ten years Molly has lived with the Hillier family and their three daughters, Caitlyn, Emily, and Jennifer, in Illinois. Molly is a small, but vigorous and strong dog that enjoys outdoor activity. Perhaps, that may be reason enough to walk with her on a nature trail in and around their town. Molly doesn't hunt foxes or badgers, yet she can kill rabbits, mice, rats, and other vermin. One day last year, she even tackled a raccoon, gripped it by its throat, and kept shaking it until it died.

On the other hand, owners of Cairns love their dogs and can fully attest to their warm personality, friendliness, and their absolute readiness to please. I know for sure since Molly and I have bonded so well during our baby-sitting visits. In order to satisfy Molly, I take her to the green trails near their home. To get Molly's immediate attention, all I need say is: "Okay, Molly! 'Tis time to go for our walk." Then she struts proudly with her tail straight up in the air while acting like a soldier on an adventurous crusade.

Indeed, Molly is very protective of her family. She is playful, alert, loyal, and loves the treats she gets after the early morning walks. We give her credit for her enthusiasm, and she will do anything to have her belly rubbed. Lately, she will bark at whatever is a threat to her loved ones. Now I know why farmers have Cairn terriers as pets, since they know they will get rid of mice, rats, or other rodents in their hay or grain. The good thing is that Cairns are doubly blessed with two coats of hair. They have a hefty, thick, woolly undercoat and, as a result, are protected against very cold temperatures. In the case of their overcoat, you may use the word "shaggy" to describe them well.

Needless to say, Christmas Day was a sad occasion. The morning started off being festive, but early in the afternoon, Molly broke away from the electric dog fence, and we spent the rest of the day searching for her. It's strange because she had her security collar on to prevent her from getting too close to the boundary line. Nevertheless, she must have gotten some kind of shock when she left the yard. The mere thought of losing Molly is much the same as losing a family member. To think that she was missing was overwhelming and incomprehensible to say the least. The actual loss made us all feel helpless, sad, and depressed. Yet we knew at the same time how many wonderful moments we spent with her. Grief was so tormenting to cope with in our family's dilemma. For sure we experienced an incredible amount of stress.

Caitlyn, our oldest granddaughter, decided to take a proactive approach to things. She made computer-generated signs which we posted all over the neighborhood. We also alerted the police for their support in such a time of dire need. In retrospect, I can hear our youngest granddaughter, Jennifer, say compassionately: "If Molly is lost for good, then I know we will find her in Heaven."

Christmas Day ended without any sign of Molly. The next morning, my two sons, George and David, and I, scoured the neighborhood and after searching for over three hours, we returned disillusioned about what may have happened to our dear Molly. Even though we are family, we still seemed all alone with our grief and in desperate need of emotional support. Later on in the afternoon, we got a call from an Asian lady who was speaking in broken English, "I found your number to call on tree. Your dog bark all night long! Me get no sleep! Come and pick dog so I can go to sleep more! Dog on deck! He still barking all time!" In the final analysis, the lady was very pleased when we gave her a reward for finding our dog—the apple of our eye.

When Molly saw us, she jumped in a frenzy of joy and we also were so happy to have her reunited with our loving family. Now it's so exciting to find life to be more sustainable by our returning to such a loving sense of peace and comfort. Outside the snow is coming down and the stubble fields are fully covered with snow swept about by the cold and desolate wind. That doesn't matter anymore for we are all home together with a blazing fire in the grate. At last, we can listen to the merry laughter that breaks the lonely stillness on such a spectacular winter's night.

THE OLD RED ROOSTER

I have a hard time explaining myself. At present, I have made a fool of myself. It's not so easy explaining a stupid thing like this, even though I was very young at the time.

I don't understand what the rooster was doing at the time. The mad look on his face was exasperating to me, as he pinned the hen to the floor of the henhouse. Perhaps I should have been privy to certain things, especially about the sexual things between a rooster and a hen.

I'm beginning to learn what it is with ants and what it looks like with them. They're going about mad, not knowing one another, nor caring, because they all seem to be looking to please the queen. I can see that certain look in their faces: some wanting and knowing they're looking for something.

Many others are looking for whatever they can find, just can't get it, are denied it, but putting up with it, just content momentarily to be discontented. I'm beginning to see the light. Yes, I'm a neophyte, but I'm getting the broader picture. What are they all looking for? Love? Happiness? I suppose it goes deeper than that— some universal thing that's wanting. I dare say

I should have been more aware of nature and the well-ordered scheme of things.

The rooster is in the hen house. I can see it all as Ralphie, cock-of-the walk, comes strutting his stuff, bides his time, and, unbeknownst to Sylvia, flutters down from his perch and lands on her and goes to town. Something tells me he knows when the time is ripe. Ralphie looks so self-assured and, perhaps, far too cocky for his own good.

I am beside myself. My heart goes out to Sylvia who is being squashed and remains prostrate with her face on the messy floor. Evidently, he's treating her like dirt; for some reason or other, I don't even hear one solitary cluck out of her. I shout at him, "Gwan outta that Ralphie!" He's too busy to pay me mind. What else can I do in such a dilemma? What's going to happen? Will Sylvia die? And will I become accessory after the fact for not having prevented her death from happening?

I try my best to push Ralphie off Sylvia, but it's like he's locked into her. Imagine that, if you will. For some strange reason, he goes about his business, completely unperturbed by my actions. I doubt even Superman can ever break his stranglehold. Whatever I do comes to no avail. I'm worried, though, if I don't do something now, I'm afraid Sylvia will surely die, after having being sandwiched between the floor boards and that unmerciful rooster.

Since Ralphie doesn't stand for reason, I tap him at first with my swagger stick. He doesn't budge. Then I add more pressure by whacking him harder. I honestly believe there's the devil in him. Mind you, he's still stuck on Sylvia, but he gets a little groggy with the force of the blows and the mortal sounds of whackety, whackety, whack, whack, whack. The blood flies everywhere. I wipe the blood stains off my stick and throw it outside. It's strange in a way; he's still on top, though it's more like he's impersonating a drunken sailor.

Suddenly, I begin to sweat profusely, for I can feel the cool drops of sweat running down my rib cage. Ralphie fights for his balance, but loses it. He looks gawky, and his body sags, but he manages to skulk to the north end of the henhouse and, for sure, away from me. I give him a little water and feed, but he looks the other way. He keels over.

I lift up his head, but his eyes open and close like window shutters dropping down over a kitchen light. I believe he narrows his eyelids to cut down the glare. He's still alive, but fading fast. I feel great guilt about the terrible accident that's happening here. The tears roll down my cheeks after witnessing such a bloody scene. Suddenly, he slumps and rolls over dead. Ralphie's eyes are closed for good.

The family rooster has bitten the dust. In retrospect, I must have hit him like he never knew what hit him. The more I stare at him, the more ashamed I am for having created such a heinous spectacle.

Here I was being a Sir Galahad, proud of my conduct, by being the noble protector of the goodness in life, no doubt, the acknowledgment of a hero. The torment inside me runs counter to the heart's core. You see I'm not the lifesaver I thought I was, but the murderer I don't wish to be. My nerves are some frayed. The only consolation is the weather is fine. Nevertheless, I'm afraid I'll always be remembered as the bloody one who killed the old red rooster on McKay Street.

My conscience gets into the act, "Imagine that, George, Ralphie no longer rules the roost."

"For Heaven's sake, I know that!"

"Another thing, George?"

"What's that?"

"And neither does he strut!"

"And you know what? No more cock-a-doodle-do."

"That's what I have to live down. Enough, enough already!"

I come out of the henhouse for it's as if the walls of this place are closing in on me. I sit on a swing, bite my lip, and kick the dirt about my feet with my black boots. I'm not in the mood for swinging. I sit and sit and stare and am overcome by life and death. In the clear air I smell the bonfire of leaves on the Dole Road sending up its incense like an afternoon's sacrifice.

Then I find a glimmer of hope as I dwell on the words of my great-grandmother, Jessie Caroline Wilcox Cassidy, who passed on these precious words to me, "Remember when something bad happens, it doesn't mean it's the end of the world. Tomorrow is a new day for you will find that you are never too old to learn and never too young to begin." O! I look up longingly to the Southside Hills, lovely beyond words, with it's tie-in with my world as I reflect upon its lesson, "I will lift up mine eyes unto the hills, from whence cometh my help." (Psalm 121:1) I meditate and wonder if things will ever get better on the other side of night.

Nevertheless, I realize this coming Sunday morning I'll be in my pew at Wesley United Church, at the proper time and place, to be among the saints and sinners, and to make atonement for killing the old red rooster, our family's own flesh and blood.

That's more than I can fathom on a day like this when I become prey to my own thoughts and dreams. The henhouse door is left open and, instinctively, I want to print big block letters above the door as a warning to everyone:

"ABANDON HOPE ALL YE WHO ENTER HERE!"

Now I must face the music and tell my mother what needs to be told.

"Mom! You're not going to like this, but I must tell you what happened."

"O, no! What next?"

"You know, Ralphie?"

"Wouldn't you believe I do? Yes!"

"You don't have to worry about him anymore?"

"What are you talking about?"

"Ralphie's dead!"

"My heavens! What happened?"

"When I opened the door of the henhouse, I saw him regally perched on Sylvia and with feathers flying about everywhere and squeezing her to death. At least, I could see he was mauling her. I thought for sure Sylvia was about to die."

"So, what did you do?"

"I wanted to see justice done. So I hammered Ralphie."

"With a hammer?"

"No! With my swagger stick. I wasn't going to stand for such ructions."

Then my mother, after the fact, enlightens me a little more about the birds and bees. At least, I'm beginning to get other ideas about the natural state of things. She can tell I was taking this disaster with the greatest amount of sympathy for the family rooster.

Later on in life, I learned a lot more about the birds and bees. I also learned why the chicken crossed the road: to have sex. How daft I used to be. I find out more dope about the well-kept secret between Ralphie and Sylvia. Ralphie mounts Sylvia who has to coopy down to endure his weight. He holds her by the feathers on her neck just behind her head. Then he tucks his tail in what is lovingly called the "cloaca kiss," thereby passing sperm to fertilize the egg before the shell goes on. Anyway, I still contend that roosters and hens still fight like cats.

'Tis my mother who comforts me. "Unfortunately, Ralphie is dead, but I know you didn't do it deliberately. So the damage is already done. There's nothing else you can do about it. I'm getting tea ready now. When your father comes home, you can straighten things out with him."

"Mom, you know there's something that appears mighty peculiar to me. I noticed when Sylvia was freed from Ralphie's bloody onslaught, she rose matter-of-factly from the floor, shook herself, unruffled her feathers, and walked nonchalantly out the door as if nothing unruly had ever happened. Can you explain it to me?"

"Yes! Yes! It's all part of nature, George. In order for us to have eggs in the morning, Ralphie has to do his thing and Sylvia has to grin and bear it. That's life, my son. That's often the way it is even with any man and his wife. Their squabble is only momentary. It's not as bad as it looks."

"It isn't?"

Outside the henhouse, I am mighty angry with the rooster and mighty angry with myself. It would have been better if I had just pulled Ralphie off Sylvia instead of hitting him with my swagger stick. I should have been more aware of the well-ordered scheme of things between a rooster and a hen. I sit on a swing, but I don't feel like swinging. My mind is not with it because it seems to want to step through the doorway of that henhouse and escape from my crime—into the sunlit air, to hear the resolute sounds of hungry gulls, see the waves crash against the rocks upon the shore, smell the sea, and, above all, find some sacred place where I can read some heartwarming poetry.

When my father comes home, I tell him the same old story and, when tears run down my cheeks, he consoles me, "Look here, son. You're making a mountain out of a mole hill. Remember this: Ralphie was no spring chicken."

"That's nice of you to say that. I don't believe, though, that Ralphie's age has much to do with the problem at hand. You're kind to put it that way. Besides, Ralphie is no chicken; he's a rooster."

"Son, we can get a new rooster. We'll miss our eggs in the morning for awhile, but you know, George, what I'll miss most of all?"

"What's that, Dad?"

"His cock-a-doodle song. His crowing in the morning was regular clockwork and just as timely as the noonday gun. Anyway, we must let bygones be bygones and get on with our lives. What else is there to do?"

"Dad, you know one thing, if Ralphie hadn't allowed his feelings to get the better of him, I believe he'd be alive today."

"You can't say that for sure. One thing about it, son, you can't beat human nature no matter how hard you try."

"As of now, I'm going to turn over a new leaf. I'll start over as if this never happened. From now on I'll try not to get into any more trouble."

"That's good news to hear, my son."

Nevertheless, I'm downright ashamed for having created such a heinous spectacle. Once in awhile, I reflect on the song that comes back to haunt me: "She'll be comin' 'round the mountain. . . ." I used to love singing that song, but when it came to "We will kill the old red rooster, when she comes," I always remain deathly quiet. I don't know, but the thought of that song is too much to handle. It's unfathomable at times to contain my secret grief and the painful reality that lies before me. That night I never spent any time counting sheep. I was possessed: in a tear over Ralphie and our family's major loss. I wake up during the night by shouting out, "You dirty dog! You shitty rooster!" I couldn't sleep and when I did, the hobgoblins make their visitation.

I'm hauled into the courthouse and appear before the judge. "What's the charge here?"

I listen to the pronouncement, "Assault with a deadly weapon, your honor, and the potential of endangering the lives of others on McKay Street."

"What is your name, young man?"

"George Hillier, yer honor?"

"How old are you?"

"Do you mean right now?"

"Well, I suppose now is as good a time as any. On the other hand, let me put it to you another way, 'When is your birthday?' "

"December 20th, yer honor!"

"Of course! But what year?"

"Every year, yer honor."

"I'm sitting here still waiting to hear the year you were born. You're wasting my good time, young man."

" 'Twas a bad year! An ignoble year. I didn't want to bring it up. It was 1929, exactly the time when my mother went into depression. You see when she told me she was depressed, it wasn't so much because of the depression in the world."

"What else could it have been?"

"She was depressed because I was born!"

"Of course, you're saying that with tongue-in-cheek."

"You got it, yer honor! It's good to laugh at life once in awhile, don't you think?"

"Yes! Of course. Where is the rooster, Master Hillier?"

"Dead now, sir!"

"Where did he go?"

"Ask me no questions and I'll tell you no lies. If there's a heaven for roosters, then he's there right now."

"Did you beat your rooster with malice of forethought?"

"Indeed, not! With me swagger stick, judge!"

"Why did you murder him?"

"I never murdered him a'tall, sir! What do you take me for? The very idea!"

"Yes, but he's dead, isn't he?"

"Well, truth to tell, he will spraddle no more."

"What do you mean by spraddle?"

"Your honor, a "rooster spraddle" is also called "A dick spraddle" which is to say finding how far a rooster can go in one leap. Look! It's as simple as that. Of course, yer honor, he's deader'n a dick. If you must know, that means he's quite dead."

"In that case, if you didn't murder him, then how did he die?"

"I just hit him with my swagger stick. That's it."

"So the murder weapon was your swagger stick?"

" 'Twas so! But why do judges always talk in a blasphemous way?"

"We don't, but in your case, we have to make some exceptions. Life is that way. So get used to it for crying out loud. Where's the weapon now?"

"I buried it in my backyard."

"You mean to tell me you buried the evidence?"

"I had nothing to hide, but I felt better if I got rid of the stick."

"So where is the rooster? Did you bury him too?"

"O! Cripes! I had to bury him. I had to get rid of the corpse."

"Why on earth would you do such a thing?"

"Yer honor, Ralphie was smelling to high heaven. There was no other recourse."

"In all sincerity, how could you have committed such a dastardly act?"

"Let me tell you, it wasn't easy. I must say 'twas strictly unintentional. If I knew Ralphie was going to die, I would not have chastised him like I did. Really, though, I don't like to take things to extreme. For the most part, I must admit, I gave him a tallywhacking."

"We don't use that word anymore, do we?"

"Why not? I just did. In fact, a swagger stick can be used for a tally stick."

"How is that possible?"

"It's easy. A tally stick can be notched to keep the counts of seal pelts or salted cod or the like."

"I know what "whacking" means, but what does "tally" mean?"

"It stands for a person with a dark complexion?"

"Can you give me an example?"

"Yes! A Tally is a St. John's citizen who is of Syrian or Lebanese descent. My good uncle, Freddy Michael, is a Tally. I never call him a Tally though. No siree! I find the word too derogatory myself. Out of respect, I prefer to call him a true Newfoundlander."

"Are you in denial, young man?"

"Of what?"

"Denial of the rooster's death?"

"Undeniably, but that doesn't make me feel any better after the fact. I want to get this clear, you're not my judge. God is my Judge. I gave Ralphie a taste of his own medicine. He deserved it."

"It looked like your rooster was smashed in the head."

"No way, yer honor. Well, in some instances I did give him some raps on the head. I hit him in other parts of the body as well. Maybe my conscience deserted me in my hour of need."

"Yes, my goodness, but how many times did you whack the rooster?"

"No more'n a dozen or so. It may even have been more or again it could have been less. 'Tis hard to say. They weren't love taps, that's for sure."

"Pray tell, how hard did you hit the rooster?"

"As God is my judge, yer honor, I hit him fairly hard as I recall."

"So we may conclude that you just upped with your swagger stick and clubbed him to death."

"There you go again with all your legalese by making things much worse than they are. I thought Ralphie could take it at the time. My God! I never thought he was going to die on me."

"So far, Master Hillier, you have given me too many excuses involved in this crime."

"Are you sure? I certainly don't look at it that way."

"You must learn here and now that of all the excuses you have made in this case, the greatest excuse is no excuse at all."

"Hmm. You're the judge, but it's still your own opinion. I feel that my personal rights have been violated since your opinion doesn't mean it's necessarily true. It's merely your opinion against mine."

"Master Hillier, do you believe in God?"

"Hello? Do I look like I don't? Ha! Certainly I do! I fear God now more than I've ever felt in all my life. I realize I lacked good judgment and hearken on the words from Ecclesiastes, 'Wisdom is better than weapons of war: but one sinner destroys much good.' On my honor, yer honor, I know the decalogue by heart. These are the basic rules that carry binding authority or, at least, should carry binding authority in the world."

"Are you aware of the commandment, 'Thou shalt not kill'?"

"I'm fully aware of it, but what I did with Ralphie was justified in this case."

"I must remind you, young man, that killing can never be justified in any case. That's for the record. Besides, you can be funny at times, but it seems you are a smart aleck."

"I am what I am and I don't contend to be perfect, but I do the best I can in most circumstances. No one on earth is going to tell me how I should run my life. I'm not the sort to cast aspersions on anyone. At least, I'm not the judge. For sure I don't play God."

"Weren't you overly vicious with your rooster?"

"That sounds horrible. In retrospect, yer honor, I never in all my born days laid a hand on Ralphie! The swagger stick's to blame. Besides, you don't say anything about Sylvia, our first rate hen, whose life I saved in due process."

"That's a likely story. It's apparent to me you are some strong for a little guy. Is that right?"

"You're partly right, but the stick helped a lot."

"Do you mind if I ask you a question?"

"You're the judge! Go ahead. I'm not going to stop you, above all people."

"Why did you lose control?"

"How can you sit there and say such a thing when you weren't even there yourself. Damn it! I never lost control. Ralphie was the one who lost control for God's sake! So there! He started it in the first place. I call it a disgraceful act on Ralphie's part. It looked like he was in a crazed mood. He was much too broody to my liking."

"The problem is you may have a mean streak in you. Am I getting close?"

"Aw, yes! Much too close for comfort, yer honor. 'Tis mostly genetic, though, for it all comes down to the last syllable of recorded time. You see, I'll have you know my fore-fathers were bona fide seal hunters and were only case-hardened enough to know what it means to have tallywacked the seals while coppying on the ice. Besides, I love flipper pie as much as I love figgy duff."

"As far as I'm concerned, you are still in denial. Now you are blaming it on heredity. Is that so?"

"All right, cookie, let me ask you, where would we be without it? Just the other day, when my mother and I were in a row, she finally gave up on me and said, 'The trouble with you is that you're just like your father's people!' If you want to know the truth, that's it in the nutshell. Not one word of a lie.' "

"So you blame it on your family tree, no doubt?"

"You got it, yer honor! Somewhere out there in Brigus, Heart's Content, and in Trinity, I'm still duty bound to track down some ancestors to find my faded genes. You see when I look up our family tree, I latch onto a few lemons, the occasional nut, and a few good apples."

"So where are you on that tree?"

"I'm the good apple most of the time. Once in awhile, I branch off as it were. On the other hand, I did go out on a limb for Sylvia's sake. At least, I know I'm not rotten to the core. You have to realize I'm still in quest of the forefather who has given me so much torment over the years. With all due respect to you, yer honor, without naming names, I know some family trees have withered 'cause nobody tends to their roots anymore."

"In the future, young man, whenever you do a hand's turn for anyone, will you do me a big favor?"

"Of course, yer honor! What's that?"

"Leave your swagger stick home! Go home now and for God's sake sin no more. Case dismissed!"

GOD SHINES HIS LIGHT UPON HER WAY

God shines His light upon her way,
Uplifts her soul at break of day;
We feed on words that purify
To hear His thoughts that glorify.
Then we know He answers her prayer.
Yes! We know He answers her prayer.

Some day before the world turns cold,
Before the years tell us we're old,
Then let us thank the Lord above
And let us praise Him for His love.
Then we know He answers her prayer.
Yes! We know He answers her prayer.

We sing for mercy, strength, and grace
When grief grows for the human race,
But we walk in His blessed sight:
The perfect way, the truth, and light.
Then we know He answers her prayer.
Yes! We know He answers her prayer.

Whenever we shall see His face
Our faith and trust in Him embrace;
We hope before our courage fails

To find His blessing still prevails.
Then we know He answers her prayer.
Yes! We know He answers her prayer.

With love and appreciation for our dear friend,
Jean Totzke, who died suddenly in 2006.

WITHOUT OUR FRIENDS

Without our friends, we'd be non-entities
For we shared with you our joy and sadness
And now it's time to give you thanks and
    praise
For yesterday, today, and tomorrow.
Whenever we settle down and listen
With open hearts and minds we hear your
    voice
For love's in the deepest well of being.
'Tis love that shapes our lives, thoughts,
    and actions
And tells us how we must think of our
    friends
Since love's the greatest miracle of all
When it comes to measuring our friendship.
Friends are firm and unwavering and
We stayed in Wisconsin because of you.

ONCE UPON A DAY

I decide to look for a job in May so I may be able to work during the summer holidays, take care of myself and prepare for some of the give-and-take of the world. Mostly, though, in the back of my mind, is the fact that I wish to help out at home. I am absolutely certain my father works too hard six out of seven days a week. Every evening, after tea, he goes down into his basement, stands forever at his bench and builds such things as cots, end tables, and bookcases for friends, relatives, and storm sashes for his mother.

Life is a matter of simple economics when mouths have to be fed. You see, when more money has to go out to pay bills, more money has to come in, and when that doesn't occur, everyone in the family must learn just how it is to do without. We are not poor exactly because we have food on the table. Of course, happiness always comes when we can afford a brick of Brookfield's Ice Cream for dessert to polish off a Sunday dinner.

In the middle of May when I was twelve, I applied for three jobs in the city. Unfortunately, these jobs had already been filled by other applicants. Then I happened to see an ad in *The*

Evening Telegram. Immediately I called Breen's Bazaar and spoke to the secretary who was kind enough to set up an appointment for me. At least that's another possibility. Though I missed out on three potential jobs with other employers, there is still a glimmer of hope.

On this day I look out the window and see dark clouds hovering over Cabot Tower on Signal Hill, and so, it appears that we'll have the same weather we had yesterday—rain, drizzle, and fog. I am to meet Mr. Breen at four o'clock in the afternoon. As I eat my porridge, I am getting to feel a little anxious. My mother seems to know what is going on in my mind. Her sense of intuition is uncanny. She helps me get ready for school, and asks me questions on geography to get set for the test in the morning. She knows that learning comes hard for me. Yet, here I am, the one who finds pride in himself as well as in his willingness to work faithfully for the family.

After eating my breakfast, my mother makes sure my appearance is presentable. She gives me a pure white handkerchief in case I should sneeze. That's one of my problems, for whenever I get nervous, I have a tendency to sneeze. She reminds me to take my raglan. She stands at the front door of the porch, kisses me good-bye and wishes me luck in my test and my interview.

As soon as I leave my house, I walk along Water Street, and whom should I see but Mrs. DeLorey, my next door neighbor. We exchange pleasantries. She is a fascinating woman, a pleasure to see. Her name is Mabel, except on our street she is nicknamed "Scotty." Jimmy, her husband, was in the First World War, wounded at Beaumont Hamel, struck-off-the strength, and is now retired. Mrs. DeLorey hails from Scotland, but after the war, Jimmy took her on as his bonny bride. This woman is all business around her house, and good-natured; she still sings as she did in her old country years ago. Her quaint face is amusing, but when she sings in the neighborhood at any seasonal event like a birthday or Christmas time, her eyes positively dance with laughter. I walk through the rain and drizzle while she puts me in a bright mood. She used to give me some old Scottish ballads and songs to remember. It took ages for me to learn them off by heart. I still remember one verse of three verses of songs she used to sing. One Scottish song comes back to me. I loved to hear her strange accents, and the way she mouthed the words as she sang this Scottish song about Mr. Raeburn, the Atheist:

" 'Twas within a hall of Rilchester town,
In the springtime of the year,

Luke Raeburn gave a lecture on
the soul of man,
And found that it cost him dear.
Windows all were smashed that day.
They said, 'The Atheist can pay.'
But Scottish Raeburn frowning cried,
'Na,na, it winna do,
I canna, canna, winna, winna,
munna pay for you.' "

Mrs. DeLorey is the sort of woman I like to meet. Although she has a long nose, it never seems to bother her because her father insisted when she was a child, that long noses were fashionable and aristocratic; ever since that day she never seemed to worry about it at all. Strangely enough, whenever she laughs, it comes suddenly and very heartily at anything that amuses her and without first smiling or suggesting by any other design that she is amused. So, I take my leave of her, and I begin to forget about myself and keep on walking to school with a laughing face.

As soon as I get to Centenary Hall School, I go down to the school yard because I have about twenty minutes before the school bell rings. I see my friend, Percy Marsh, and we get to skylarking. He wrestles me and in an instant throws me to the ground. He does that to me three times in a row. He is much stronger than I.

I know how fast he is too, and I have great respect for his running ability. I ask him, "Look, Percy, how about a race across the yard to the red fence? Why don't we see if we can come in together?" He agrees. In the meantime I am nervous in case he may beat me. We shout out to one another, "On your mark! Get set! Go!" Percy gets off to a fast start, slows a little so we can come in together in a dead heat, but I catch up with him and pass him handily toward the red fence. Of course, he is disgusted with me. "I thought we agreed to finish together. What happened?"

"I guess I must have gotten nervous," was all I had to say.

As soon as I get to my desk, I notice a Canadian Red Cross poster on the wall. There is a picture of a boy on it, and he is in the process of sneezing. The caption reads, "When you cough, or sneeze, or sniff, always use a handkerchief!"

The good thing about school today is that I don't have to stay after for extra help. We had our classes in art, handwriting, arithmetic, geography, history, and literature. I may have passed my geography test, but I don't know. I do believe I should have studied my material longer so the facts would have been clearer in my mind. Although, when I read my geography book, I get caught up with not only the letters and words, but I also get plagued with the dots above the letter "i's," the commas, and the periods. Miss Butt, my teacher, says, "You can see the trees, but you get stumped in the forest." When she explained this thought to me, I could not have agreed with her more. It is true I read at a snail's pace when everyone else has already finished the story; I look back and ask myself, "How much can I recall?" Art is another subject that baffles me. I am embarrassed to think about the limitations I have in this subject. I just cannot draw, and when I do draw something or other, I don't want anyone to see it. In fact, I tear it up in a jiffy. Even when I attempt to draw a straight line, it ends up crooked.

Larry Winsor, however, is another story. He is brilliant in art. I believe he can work a master-piece in his sleep. He has a flair for drawing anything under the sun or over the moon. I am impressed with the perfection of his art-work. Yet by the same token, he is one of the poorest pupils in the class. I cannot figure it out. This is where I have it over him a little. His main love is art, but his worst one is arithmetic, since he has trouble with multi-plication and especially his times table. He is pleased to know, though, that I am his fan when it comes to admiring his art. He con-fides in me about his shortcomings in school,

"When it comes to learning and gettin' it, I have trouble gettin' it! It seems to me I have to pull myself up by my own bootstraps."

I sit in a double desk with my first cousin Fred Coaker, who is a good listener and catches on quickly, although he is not always motivated. During recess, he has his greatest moments. With no thought of gain or fame, Fred is literally some kind of magician. For example, he pulls his lower lip up until it stretches beyond the bridge of his nose. I smile at his magic. I cannot separate myself from the feeling of awe about him. Another time Howie Sparks plays a stunt which is like playing a cruel game to his detriment. He takes a Gillette blue blade from his desk and places it carefully into his mouth that he widens for the occasion. He makes sure his tongue doesn't get caught in the action. When he begins to do this, sudden fear and emotions rise up inside of me. I cannot forget that such a ritual unfolds in front of me. I'm some sure my face must have a haunted look. He chews the blade very carefully and is precise about not swallowing any left-over matter. Finally, his teeth break the blade into small fragments. He spits them out of his mouth without having cut himself. I ask him to open his mouth so everyone can notice his teeth are milky white and, above all, undoubtedly every tooth is geometrically square. That is one feat for *Ripley's Believe It or Not.* Another popular stunt is when he swallows fire. To complicate matters, Howie takes a sheet of scribbler paper, crumples it, lights a Sea Dog match to it, and then puts the flame into his mouth.

Howie, for all that, is a sensitive person who blinks his eyes a mile a minute while at the same time, he grins constantly even when no one is looking. Yet he was an important friend when we went to school and experienced the longest days and the shortest nights.

Some good things are better left last like literature, my favorite subject in school. We had to read orally one of William Butler Yeats' poems. To tell the truth, this one, "The Lake Isle of Innisfree" is my all-time favorite for its sensitivity, its love of nature, and above all, its love of life when every word springs up at you so sentimentally. It's a poem, but when you sound out the words, you will hear music, and the song will come to you.

"I will arise and go now, and go to Innisfree,
And a small cabin build there,
of clay and wattles made,
Nine bean rows will I have there,
a hive for the honeybee,
And live alone in the bee-loud glade.

And I shall have some peace there,
for peace comes dropping slow,
Dropping from the veils of the morning
to where the cricket sings,
There midnight's all a glimmer,
and noon a purple glow,
And evening full of the linnet's wings.

I will arise and go now, for always
night and day.
I hear the lake water lapping with
low sounds by the shore,
While I stand on the roadway,
or on the pavements grey,
I hear it in the deep-heart's core."

I come out of school and head for my appointment. As I walk, I am saying I shall do my best, supposing I succeed or fail. I pass the house where a man I knew used to live. This is where the Jamiesons live. I know why the window blinds are down at that house. In the city, or anywhere around the bay, when anyone dies, the standard custom is to pull down the blinds, shut the world outside, so the mourners can find some peace and quiet within.

Just down a ways houses are joined together like a long funeral. The people looking like bodies jammed in prisons are huddled together—the Horde of The Grateful Poor.

With their clothes torn and patched, nothing seems to bother them for the most part. I see one woman with her jaws chewing hard and her eyes soft and brilliant. When I see those poor, no matter how futile you may think their lives are, they go in search for their daily rounds of pleasure. Indeed, they will take their chance on happiness. One boy comes out, and he looks much too thin to my liking. He runs and is dressed up in his father's khaki coat and, being stimulated by the cool air, marches like a soldier with nervous energy and thinks to himself about the blessedness of his own dreams. I walk along and in the distance I hear the voice of a baby crying.

Further down the street the complexion of the houses changes. I see to the right of me a grand house where Gloria Wellstone lives. I know her, but she doesn't know me, or pretends she doesn't know me or, even if she does know me, she never speaks to me. That's all right. That's the way it is. Gloria is a Newfoundlander who goes to school in England, so her parents can guide her along the paths of greater usefulness. I can hear her speaking to her mother in a British accent, "Please mother, heat the rolls and pass the serviettes!"

Out of consciousness of time and place as an onward Christian soldier, I pass by my church, Wesley United, the sacred place that means so much to me. You see, that's the only place where I can find out whatever I can about the secret yearning of the heart. I do believe in striving for someone above me, because I can't make it alone. There in that holy place I am intent and I am in search to find as much as I can about this holy scatterer of daily bread. Believe you, me, I am the veritable shy one, who learns so much about God, The Good Shepherd, who makes such marvelous use of the imagery of Darkness and Light. Whilst there, I smile down from my pew upstairs and keep my eyes peeled on the hygienic faces of the orphanage girls who get to stir me up inside. O! I am waiting for the man I used to call "God," the Reverend Armitage, and I am surely captivated as he goes on,

"And God shall wipe away all tears from
their eyes; and there shall be no more death,
neither sorrow, nor crying, neither shall
there be any more pain: for the former things
are passed away . . . Behold, I make all
things new . . . I am Alpha and Omega,
the beginning and the end."

Oh verily, verily, I hear him talk about believers, for sure, and there's no nonsense about him. He tells us to find our new Heaven and Earth in this city of ours. He proclaims we have to be true believers. We have to be ready at a moment's notice, since we may have to surrender ourselves to the God up above in famine or in nakedness or in suffering or in distress, because He is the Great Wondrous Light of the World. I am always touched by his sermons, just as I am fascinated by the words and musical names of the Indians from Longfellow's "Hiawatha" which we are learning in our school.

Whoever walks Water Street is bound to run into the likes of Eldred Holwell. He is the consummate zoot suiter. I see him on the sidewalk smoking his Royal Blend cigarette and, summarily, doubting it with his rotating foot before he enters Ayre & Sons Store. He is the floorwalker, the genial one, who makes your life worthwhile and knows exactly how to break up your moments of silence. As the story goes, he announces to the other clerks to get their attention: "B'y, I'm some proud because Mr. Ayre spoke to me today." The clerks listen to Eldred, but they pay him no heed. One of the clerks gets frustrated and loses his patience and speaks to Eldred, "We know, Mr. Ayre. We know he stands for no nonsense. He speaks to God, speaks to the missus, and speaks to no one else!" Yet for all that, Eldred's persuasion becomes irresistible, "I'm telling ye! Mr. Ayre spoke to me today!"

The selfsame clerk, moving his hands about in a gesture of helplessness, starts to yield, "OK Eldred. If Mr. Ayre spoke to you today, what did he say?" Eldred grins and laughs. He said, "GET OUT OF MY WAY!"

At Adelaide Street I come across Billy Shea, the one-time Irishman who is nicknamed "The Harp Wot Got Da Yarns." You may have read "Jack and the Beanstalk," but I dare say you may not have heard the story with the Irish slant:

"I do believe, yerra, what a sort of feller, queer lookin' and stunned-like Jack were, after all, a good-for-nuttin' bum. An' a bung eye he was after gettin' not from de giant but from his mudder because he were asleep, and she couldn't raise the bugger from de dead. He and his mudder only had one cow between their selves. An wot o' dat, to be sure! Jack did everything back formass, for wot, I dunno. An' Lord God o' Heaven, they didn't know if the cow were a Kerry or were a Donegal. An' God a mercy, they didn't know der beans like I knows dem. They didn't know the broad ones from the scarlet runners."

The secretary, Miss Jacobs, tells me that Mr. Jeremiah Breen is busy, but will be along shortly. "Anyway," she says in a nice way, "he knows about your appointment." I tell her that I am quite early, and I just want to be sure that I get here early enough so there'll be no problem with being late.

I take the skull cap off my head, sit down and place the cap on my right knee to cover up the worn-out patches of my green corduroy breeks. I sit demurely. My face is scrupulously clean, and my black wavy hair is slicked back with Vaseline Hair Tonic no less, and my black boots are shined up with Nugget Polish. I hope I am presentable enough. I have on green woolen stockings, breeks, and khaki shirt my mother made for me, and a brown suede jacket my mother bought me on The Installment Plan at The Royal Stores. I hope Mr. Breen does not get too mesmerized by my two front teeth that are pockmarked in the middle. I am, I must remind you, the shy one, the twillick, but outside of that, I am honest, courageous, firm, steady, straightforward, and hardworking, because if you don't have such qualities, you can't compete in this life.

There's something about going for an interview. You have no idea what's going to happen. The pressure is on. I swear it's the same as being on trial. For awhile I keep my hands folded together for consolation. I am deep in thought about something or other, no matter what it is. I close my eyes momentarily because I'm nerved up today.

While I wait on and on, time seems to stand still. Even seconds don't pass away quickly enough for me. I don't know why, but I begin counting upwards to one hundred or more. I feel the beads of sweat run down my rib cage. My eyes are next taken up with a Tiffany lamp that is hanging from the office ceiling. The picture before me is extraordinary, a vision of exquisite and unearthly colored beauty stunning my eyes.

I still have a lot of time to go. I get restless and stand up and walk over to a picture window that is opposite to where I have been sitting. In the splendid circumstance of my tea-and-bread-and-butter days, I look out the window and I see everything perfectly clear. The ritual is unfailing, and I am much moved. I see the city rising above the foreign faces of sailors, and I begin to wonder whether or not the city can feel at home where all the surroundings of life seem to be changing so fast.

I see below me the blue and white dancing waves, and I see the spray on city's eyes, the salt upon its lips. I see the grey wooden wharves below Water Street, and I see ships anchored there just to make me giddy. I see busybodies and the gossip gets through to everybody. I see the Cabot Tower up above me on a lonely hill, the tower they should have named after Marconi. Pray tell, who is the anonymous one in the city who used to say, "If you can see the Cabot Tower, it's a sign of rain. If you can't see it, it's already raining." I see the longshoremen smiling all around and cracking jokes, and waiting for more ships.

I see the sunshine and shadows falling down upon the crazy-looking fishing flakes, defying gravity; these flakes hang on for dear life among the multitudes of ancient scabrous rocks. I see all over the blue sky and the Southside Hills where I go to pick partridge berries for my mother in summertime. I see all that and I see more. I see the hovering gulls, and I hear their crying eyes. As the past returns to the present, I see Sir Humphrey Gilbert, never wanting for ambition, running on an errand for Queen Elizabeth, and all dressed up in women's clothes. I see him sail proudly into Saint John's Harbor to claim Hell's Half Acre for England. Lastly, I see Sir Humphrey sailing for home and disappearing into the Atlantic Ocean like a rabbit down a hole. I see the tide, and I see once the tide comes in, I know because I know enough to know the tide has teeth. The wind goes cool to the feeling till I come to realize the vision haunts me everywhere.

Once I leave the window I still have more

time to go. I turn around to return to my chair, but before I do, I stop to take a gander at a bulletin board. The cork board is full of sundry items. On the top left is a small statue of Jesus Christ impaled upon a cross; on the other side of the board for a sense of balance is a small statue of the Virgin Mary. Who was it who took it upon himself to utter such vaunting words as I read on the board?

"Oh! If I were queen of France, or still
     better, Pope of Rome,
I'd have no fighting men abroad,
No weeping maids at home.
All should be at peace, or
If Kings must show their might,
Why, let them who make the quarrel be.
Were only kings themselves to fight,
There'd be an end to war."

I surmise Mr. Breen must be some serious about his Roman Catholic faith. Then I begin to worry. I ask myself, "Why would Mr. Breen wish to hire a Protestant when he can get someone of his own persuasion?" I am perplexed. Most merchants in the city accept creed as a giant step toward getting a job. There are snaps of boys dressed up in their sporting uniforms representing the parochial schools such as Saint Patrick's, Holy Cross, and Saint Bonaventure.

I know how fierce the rivalry is among parochial schools in the old city. The boys from Basilica are indefatigable victors, but should they begin to lose, then their stubbornness sets in. Amidst such conflict, I am reminded of their spirit like the spirit of the grand King of Ireland, who in A.D. 537 calls out to his warriors, "Bury me," he says, "standing in my grave with me face to the north, and with me spear and me shield in my hands for as long as I stand facing them, the English cannot gain the mastery."

While there is some time left, I wonder what the dickens sort of man Mr. Breen is, anyway. My conscience disturbs me until I heed my mother's last words to me, "All you must do is be your natural self. If that doesn't work, nothing will." I know she wants me to listen carefully, since I have the strange habit of being the "World's Worst Listener."

Finally, outside the office door I hear foot-steps coming near. The door opens and in comes Mr. Breen. He is a tall man, well over six feet, heavy set, about two hundred pounds more or less. He is dressed in a gray herring-bone double-breasted suit with a gold watch with its chain visible from his vest pocket. His face is closely shaved. In fact, there are several bloody nicks that justify the closeness of his shave. He is suntanned. His eyes are keen and blue. His nose is kindly proportioned to his face, and his mouth is a little larger than normal; at least, it is filled with fairly-well formed teeth. I know when he smiles, his eyes light up accordingly.

He is accompanied by a walking cane, no doubt, to lend support to his towering structure.

I stand up sprightly as soon as Mr. Breen enters. I look into this stranger's face, and he looks into mine. As we shake hands, he buries mine. He speaks briefly to Miss Jacobs, bursts out laughing at something or other, and then sits down at his mahogany desk. He smiles ingratiatingly and tells me to bring my chair over in front of his desk. As I observe his smile, it disarms me like a remedy coming in the nick of time.

"Hello there. What is your name?"

"George Hillier, sir."

"What grade are you in?"

"Grade six, sir!"

"Do you like school?"

"Yes, sir, but learning comes hard. My problem is I have to read everything twice. Once to get used to the words and once more to understand what they're all about. Though I'm a slow learner, my teacher says I'm beginning to show more interest in my work and that progress is on the way."

"You're not discouraged, are you?"

"Not a'tall! I love my teacher who never gives up on the likes of me."

"That's good to hear young man. I appreciate your honesty."

Still when Mr. Breen and I talk to each other, our eyes meet, there is something about the two of us talking there together, and I daresay I may fancy things, since I become aware of that sort of feeling you get in the air when employer and employee begin to click.

Finally, we get back on track and he tells me that I am the third and final interview he has made to decide who will get the job. He tells me I must be responsible for such things as sweeping the sidewalk in the morning, taking down the shutters on the store windows and stashing them in the alley between Renouf's Haberdashery and Breen's Bazaar. I must also keep the store spic and span, help out the clerks, run errands, keep the bathroom as clean as possible, put the rubbish out, shine Mr. Breen's shoes twice a week, keep tabs on the twine and wrapping paper, and on each Friday morning, I must buy a codfish and bring it up to the Crossroads where the Breens live. He tells me I must work from Mondays to Saturdays from eight-thirty in the morning to six o'clock at night with one hour for dinner. In other words, I do believe Mr. Breen wants to make me generally useful.

"Now that you have a good idea of what your responsibilities must be, are you still interested in taking this job?"

"O! Yes, sir! Everything is first rate. If I get this job, then I will work tooth-and-nail for you, Mr. Breen. Guaranteed!"

"Now I ask you. Is there anything else?"

"Yes, sir there is one thing more."

"What is that?"

"It's a matter of wages, sir!"

"Well, how much are you worth?"

"I don't know, Mr. Breen. How much will you give me?"

"Well, business is getting a little better, so I can afford to pay you five dollars and twenty-five cents per week." Then he asks me summarily, "How is that for beginners, Master Hillier?"

"That's great, sir! That suits me fine and dandy."

"All right, we are all set. Welcome aboard! The job's yours."

I fill out a form on particulars for Miss Jacobs, and she speaks to me cheerfully, "Congratulations! Mr. Breen told me you got the job."

I had a great summer working at Breen's Bazaar. I appreciate the fact that the boss was considerate towards me as well as to everyone. When any of us had a birthday, he would set up a card table at the back of the store where anyone during their leisure time could share in lemon crystals and gingerbread. We always remember such generous niceties.

Although I wanted to work hard, I wanted more than anything else to please Mr. Breen more and more. So, everything I was supposed to do, I did and more. I whirled through his basement like a promise to be fulfilled. To me it was a fire hazard with old paint cans and all those oily rags around the dirt floor. I threw out boxes, pallets, two oars almost wholly consumed by termites, a metal tennis racquet, and piles of newspapers, both the *Daily News* and *Evening Telegram*. Inside three weeks I set a trap, and killed four huge harbor rats. I picked them up by their large tails and put them in a brown paper bag and disposed of them. I did have a terrible time sneezing, since I couldn't see the basement for dust. I had to clean out my nostrils as well as wash my eyes and eyelashes before they could return to normal.

I dusted the ceiling and the whitewashed walls. Dust bane helped keep down the dust while I swept the basement scrupulously clean. I didn't let on to Mr. Breen what I had done so it would come later as a pleasant surprise.

The bathroom was something else. It smelled to high heaven because the canvas around the toilet was usually damp and smelly from eternal flushings. The toilet leaked perhaps because the flush ball in the maple tank high up on the wall may not have been balanced properly. There was an ancient porcelain bathtub there with brassy lion's paws. The cold water tap was leaking a bit. So much for the pull chain toilet; I had no idea about how to fix the plumbing, but I did ask Mr. Breen if my father could repair the toilet so it would run better.

"Sir, the toilet in the bathroom is in a bad way! I know one thing, sir, if anyone can fix that for you, my father can."

"Well, thank you for reminding me. I know something should be done about it. Well, then have your father take a look at it and see what he can do."

Within a few days, my Dad came by shortly after the Noon-Day Gun. My father shook Mr. Breen's hand and told him matter-of-factly, "Mr. Breen, your toilet is in a sorry state. 'Tis on its last legs. I can fix everything for you, but to tell you the truth, I'm afraid it would only be temporary. It might be better to put in a new system."

My father did a marvelous job with the plumbing, and I could see how grateful Mr.

Breen was in this instance and paid him for the good work he had done.

The bathroom was messy when I first saw it, but having painted the ceiling, the walls and woodwork with a light glossy green color, it looked much more welcoming. Mr. Breen complimented me, "This is the cleanest this place has ever been to my knowledge. And what's more, I'm so pleased that your father did such a fantastic job." The boss's praise was all I wanted to satisfy my mind.

What I noticed in the store was a special kind of harmony. Everyone did everything to secure the goodwill of the shopper. I can see my boss now, his versatile Adam's apple moving up and down his neck, saying to his staff, "You have to satisfy the shopper, and that is, above all, the chief aim of every clerk at Breen's Bazaar." Every once in a while he would give pep talks on the psychology of sales. In order to stress the value of sales, he would put his ideas together, write them down on a piece of paper, and then Miss Jacobs would type them on official stationery. There would be a copy on the bathroom wall, so you can read some tidbits along with your morning constitutional. Other copies would be pinned on the wall behind each clerk's counter so they may read it during their spare time. This is the list of his most important objectives:

Message to Garcia:

- You must have accurate knowledge of the line of goods you sell.
- You must be able to impart your knowledge to your customers logically and quickly.
- You must possess tact to a high degree. If you are dealing with a quarrelsome buyer, don't get argumentative yourself. Using your tact may prevent a clash of minds. It may also end up in a sale. In other words, avoid a tit-for-tat mentality.
- Apply your sense of courage to any customers who may get indifferent or antagonistic. Your courage, along with your tact, and determination, may help to change their mental attitudes.
- You must be endowed with a sufficient imagination so you as a seller can put yourself in a buyer's shoes.
- Your personality plays an important role in sales. Empathy will always remain a vital part of your personality.
- You must be industrious to succeed. Even when odds go against you, your self control and willpower will help you go far at Breen's Bazaar.
- Avoid anxiety and apprehension in sales or

else you may become like a missing piece in a picture puzzle.

- Dress up in your best attire since appearance will pay its dividends. As you are, bequeath to your customer an eye-to-eye contact and a never-say-die attitude.

Remember life is a game and you are its most important player.

"If you ever lose a precious sale, it's not the end of the world nor is it the end of the rainbow. You don't have to do a song and dance. By all means, don't take it to heart. Mind you, no one is going to complain when you do your level best. There's always room here for you at Breen's Bazaar. You are still the privileged one."

A SWIMMER'S WINTRY DAY IN BOSTON HARBOR

In February of 1977, I decided to break through the ice in Boston Harbor since I heard so much about the L Street Brownies which is the oldest "polar bear" swim club in America. Of course, I was a marathoner in America and Canada, and so I decided to take on another challenge and then write about my experience for the Boston Globe. I trained for this event for two months so I'd be prepared for such an onslaught. It seems like it's a crazy thing to do; on the other hand, I felt the adrenalin flow:

Are you prepared for the swim today,
to brave the attacks of the cold wind's spray?
Irresistible force, what's come over me,
fast breaking the ice to meet the sea?

Biting blue lips and patting numb ears,
taming the sting of Neptune's icy spears.
The heart's a drum in staccato beat,
muscles and bones ache from head to feet.

As the wind's blasts blow so cruel and bold,
the stomach shakes, hands and feet grow cold;

slapped all by the waves icing the brow,
no frost, no snow can defeat me now.

The sea licks a frail body with its coarse tongue,
swimming in frigid water for just so long;
body instantly shrivels, a loss of pride,
whate'er went before turns inward to hide.

Muttering, stuttering, fluttering about,
God help me! Rush me home, thaw me out.
Just a bird quaking in a snow-filled nest,
the storm that chills may soon be lured to rest.

Eager-eyed, half-frozen, upward I spring,
the tide laps and sways, flocking seagulls sing.
Brutal fierce pangs; the sea with its clout,
an entrance, an exit, so good to be out.

A muted shriek soon razes within me:
Why do you tempt this ruthless rugged sea?
It's the fight, the spirit, one's challenge in life
to endure some pain, to belittle all strife.

This may then be the last time for me.
Never this again! Well, just wait and see.
The weather: from now on I'll not complain
of the element's ache: wind, snow, or rain.

GREAT EXPECTATIONS

At the age of 15, I saved up enough shillings to take Doreen to the Nickel Theatre in St. John's, Newfoundland. I saw her once and once was enough for me, yet I was head-in-heels in love with her even though she never knew everything about me.

She lived on the Higher Levels, and I lived on the Lower. When I think of her, I am excited and my lips are kind of twisted into a faint half-smile. The acute problem is that I have to phone her first to find out whether or not she'll go out with me.

When it comes to courting, I don't have a clue how I must behave, especially in learning about love and all its strange doings. I wonder: how long will it take to summon up enough courage to ask her for a date?

Four months later she consented, and we did see a movie. I held her hand very carefully, and as the movie was proceeding, I heard out of nowhere a girl shouting out to her boyfriend, "Take your hand off my leg or I'll call out your name!" I was more embarrassed for Doreen than I was for myself.

I was much too nervous to know what the movie was about, though I remember its title was "The Man Who Came to Dinner" starring Monty Woolley. We had a snack at Diana Sweets, and we seemed to have gotten along well together.

As we were eating, when spring comes with all its wonder, I couldn't keep my eyes off Doreen for she was a beauty if ever there was one. I was so shy that I never said a word since I was tongue-tied. I never saw such gorgeous eyes that seem to pierce me through—enough to turn my face beet red.

In my predicament, I would start to heave a few deep sighs to pass the time away. As much as my mind was working overtime, I felt so awkward and could never get the hang of being with girls. For sure they were always safe with me.

The only thing I learned about having five sisters in my family was what I derived from reading books like *The Bobbsey Twins* or playing skip rope with them or jacks. As we walked up Freshwater Road, I was getting mighty nervous for I was sweating inside and out.

First, I was worried about what God would do with me if I yielded to temptation. I know for sure He would hang me up by the "you-know-what." Second, I would never disobey my mother. I can hear her say: "Remember, son, wherever you go, don't go too far." I responded, "Mom, I'm only going to the Nickel Theatre for crying out loud!"

"That's not what I mean, son! Just treat Doreen as if she is your own sister and leave it at that." At the time, all I could say was, "I know, Mom."

Subsequently, we landed at Doreen's door, and we lingered in the porch for awhile. I felt like I could willingly die a martyr if I could only get a kiss from her. Somehow my conscience worried about what might happen at this time.

Overall, I was mighty fearful of love, the agony of its struggle, and yet I couldn't control the wild beating of my heart in the name of love. At long last I was preparing to say good-night and kissed her on the forehead. At least, I thought that was good enough for starters.

So far, so good. Somehow I wasn't quite fulfilled and leaned up against her body with the intent of kissing her on the cheek. Well? Of all things, Doreen threw her head back proudly, put her hand in front of my face and said in a matter-of-fact way, "George, I must tell you that I don't kiss on the first date."

I was hurt as if my heart was going to burst by the coolness of her words. Nevertheless, I simply had to respond as gallantly as I could by saying to her, "In that case, Doreen, can I come back tomorrow night?"

VALENTINE

O! The times you have waked
here and the moods,
wondering: when will
the heart shine, if at all,
on a gray day, and cold?
Sometimes 'tis time
to render the night
invisible. Yet the miracle
of the night is hope, lying
in winter's hibernation.
Let me tell you
there is nothing like
a heart when it is good
and right. It demonstrates
to make its color felt:
fair-folding of line.
Who told the mountains
to rise? The seas to roll?
Who told the heart
to rule till it gratifies?
Love craves the sweetness
of it in others. Besides,
what this strange place
possesses is not the cold
peace of undisturbed stones,
not the vulnerable silences,

not yet the dissolution,
but something you tell
in a story, in a song.
'Tis love, all right,
questioning the heart,
love waiting, love being,
but love giving the only
answer it can give.

A SERMON ON JOHN NEWTON: THE MAN WHO WROTE "AMAZING GRACE"

"I will not leave you desolate, I will come to you. Yet a little while, and the world will see me no more, but you will see me; because I live, you will also." John 14:18-19.

I'm not interested this morning in glorifying the present or in extolling the future, but I am interested in returning to the past. How false would our lives be if it were not for the true remembrance of years that have left their impression? After all, the past has made us what we are.

So I want to tell you now about a man who was such a blessing to the world, a man who has left a monument for all of us to behold. This man was John Newton who was born in London, England, on July 24, 1725.

John was a bright boy who could read the catechism, hymns, and a variety of poetry when he was only four years old. His mother kept a clean home and devoted herself to religious service and the raising of her son. She had great hope for his future and felt that John was clever, serious, and so very thoughtful.

He loved his mother but feared his father, a sea captain, who used to be away for long periods of time. Unfortunately, when he was only seven, his mother died of tuberculosis. Her death had left an indelible mark upon him, for he was saddened that his mother could never come back and fearful when he knew that his father would.

Lost without his mother, he had to live in a world where the strong showed little mercy for the weak. The harshness of his father, typical of fathers in those days, led to John's greater aggressiveness, for often he was too reluctant to do what he was asked. Captain Newton found his son rather difficult to handle and thought he was lazy and wasted his time even when he was occupied with books.

His school years were sometimes happy, but often it was the common fate of most pupils to be treated cruelly at school. John Newton was by no means an exception. When he finally left school, his father placed him aboard a Mediterranean ship that was to sail to Venice. He spent ten years of his life at sea and, as captain of his ship, he used to sail from England with exports to Africa and bartered these goods for black slaves who were then taken to the West Indies and America.

After that, he would sail back to England with such provisions as cotton, sugar, tobacco, and rum. While on the seas Newton wrote his own prayers for the sailors and tried to adapt the *Book of Common Prayer* to suit the crew. At one time while he was praying for a safe voyage, his sailors were contemplating mutiny. He doled out lashes from a cat-o'-nine tails for those who committed offenses and came to use thumbscrews only as a last resort.

Was there a kind of hypocrisy when Newton had prayers for a blessing on voyages which had the enslavement of human beings as a prime target? No. He did not question the slave trade then, for it was a natural part of the order of things and just as natural as three children who died in every four in infancy.

We must not forget that John lived in hard times when every village in England had its whipping post and when the penalty for shop lifting was generally death.

Another woman entered his life while Newton was deep into the slave trade. Her name was Mary Catlett, and he fell in love with her. He lacked self-confidence, however, and when it was time to propose, this man with the taste for well-turned phrases and sensitivity for verse became tongue-tied.

His heart was so full that it beat and trembled so no words could come out. Instead of saying to Mary, "I love you," he would write letters to her that went like this one, written in January, 1744:

"When I consider that though my well meaning sincerity should meet a repulse, it might one time in the power of artifice to impose on your generous, unsuspecting temper, and that I may not lose, but may perhaps lose you to a villain without a heart to value, or treat you as he ought; I can't help being doubly uneasy. The first day I saw you I began to love the thoughts of one day meriting you, so I roused from a dull insensible melancholy I had contracted, and pushed into the world. Had it not been for you, I had till this time remained heavy, sour, and unsociable."

Although Mary was not always sure what John Newton was saying, he must have gotten his point across because, finally, they saw eye to eye and were married in February, 1750.

There were times, however, when he was eager to re-examine his faith, and he began to feel a sudden remorse for his share in the slave trade. He was pleased that God had seen the danger of his voyages and spared him. Perhaps, he reflected, God is the one who was really merciful to repentant sinners.

He began to struggle to get rid of his deep-rooted sins, and although he became depressed beyond common wretchedness, he managed to hang on with grim tenacity. He always had compassion and was only looking for forgiveness. Until change came, it was his conscience that checked his humility.

He stood in need of an almighty savior because he was no longer an infidel and wanted to renounce his past sins. Delivered from the power and domination of sin, it was the grace of God that preserved him from his life of disgrace.

It was finally time to give up his trials on the seas, and he decided to make some changes. Some of his friends asked him to become a preacher, but his thoughts of the past filled him with such shame that he was reluctant to consent, but he did think about it with humility. How could he become a preacher when he had sinned so deeply and had been so blasphemous?

At first, he found it no easy matter to assure himself that such a wretch as he had been should be admitted through those heavenly gates where no impure thing could enter. Two archbishops and a bishop had refused him ordination. But his quest to serve the Lord had never weakened.

Consequently, in 1764, John Newton became the curate of the Church of England at Olney. When he preached his first sermon, he had trouble. Although he was fully prepared, he had no notes, had announced his text confidently: "I have set the Lord always before me, because He is at my right hand, I shall not be moved," yet after a few more sentences he was moved, lost his nerve, and could say no more. The very next time he preached, he wrote every word down and kept his eyes riveted to the text in case he would look off and lose his place again. Such contemporaries as George Whitefield, and the Wesleys, John and Charles, were accustomed to this and so were the congregations.

A popular preacher could preach for two hours and still maintain his sense of popularity. Two sentences on a panel in his vicarage kept him in touch with the past:

"Since you were precious in my sight, you have been honorable. But you shall remember that you were a bondman in the land of Egypt, and the Lord thy God redeemed you."

Was this the man who wrote countless hymns and prayers in seeking refuge in the power and compassion of God's love?

Was this the man who took on board ship brooding slaves, in their snuffed-out dreams, who were singing the saddest songs that no white man could ever understand?

Was this the man who was blind until he saw in time the wondrous beauty of a world that had burst upon him once he believed?

Was this the man who felt certain hunger borne out of all hope and despair, but knew that God's love would take over when the greatest sorrow had come from a sinful heart that asked forgiveness?

Was this the man whose message shone in brilliance when each word sparkled in its blessing by sounding the notes to our ears from the far corner of his sunlit world?

Was this the man who wanted us to know that we can still sing praises unto the Lord with gratitude and trust for our existence, for health, love, friendship, and for happiness in our lives?

Was this the man? Oh, yes, indeed, John Newton was truly that man.

Eventually, John became a bishop and as the good shepherd of his flock on a Sunday morning, he cared for them by helping to meet their material as well as their spiritual needs. He was, perhaps at times, a little too lenient towards their sins. He tried to rescue anyone who cried out for help. One parishioner's house burned down, and he congratulated him because he had treasure stored up in heaven that fire could never tear down. A woman came to him and said that she had just won on a lottery ticket. His reply was, "Madam, as for a friend under temptation, I will pray for you."

Those who were in spiritual trials came to

refresh their bodies in the sea or country air. When he found that some of his parishioners were not getting along, he said, "Do you reflect that another Christian may be doing God's work, though his mode of doing it may not meet your taste, any more than your taste meets his?"

When the Reverend John Newton was at Olney, he met William Cowper, and together they wrote the famous book of Olney Hymns. In this book, Newton had written 280 hymns and Cowper, 68. John Newton's hymns were a source of strength and delight, expressing profound knowledge of the heart in giving much solace for any anxious souls.

There is no reference to Hell, but much that tells of salvation from sin, mercy, and the love of Jesus Christ. Some good examples of his hymns are "Glorious Things of Thee Are Spoken," "How Sweet the Name of Jesus Sounds," and, above all, the truth and beauty of "Amazing Grace."

Cowper's hymns, on the other hand, had a melancholy strain in them, but "Oh, For a Closer Walk with God" expressed great hope and confidence. Cowper, though, had an unusual form of religious melancholia. He tried to commit suicide with poison, by drowning, by stabbing and lastly, by hanging. William, however, was not too efficient at practical matters and ended up with his body intact, for the moment anyway, but his mind was still scattered.

Hundreds of thousands of their hymns were printed and sold in the United States as well as in England. Bishop Newton was concerned with the social conditions in England, with the war with the American colonies, and with the constant increase of taxes and high price of food.

He felt that politics was "the pit that will swallow up the life and spirit." He used to say, "From poison and politics, good Lord deliver me." He tried to offer his congregation enjoyment, encouragement, and the spirit of hope.

In cooperation with a William Wilberforce, prime mover in abolishing the slave trade, John Newton wrote a confession saying that slavery was "a commerce so iniquitous, so cruel, so oppressive, and so destructive."

When his wife, Mary, died of cancer on December 15, 1790, he felt as if he were drawing near the last scene of the final act. He was besieged by grief that lasted the rest of his days and in his tranquility wrote the finest poems and hymns. He had known something of the evil of life and had enjoyed some of the good.

We can learn so much from this man, for

he wanted us to know that we should choose what we want to do with our lives, but he also wanted us to remember that the choice can make all the difference. This man had the right kind of ecumenical spirit, because he could have been at home in any church and was never interested in riches; he had discovered such wealth in his light, love, and liberty that stayed with him to the end.

When his memory was nearly gone, he could still remember two points: one was that he was a great sinner and two, that Christ was a great Savior. It was in October, 1806, that he gave his last sermon, and his cause at that time was to rescue those who were victimized at the Battle of Trafalgar.

He was aware that people were usually curious about the last words of a believer, and he said, "Tell me not how the man died, but how he lived." His will stated that: "I commit my soul to my gracious God and Savior who mercifully spared me from the state of misery on the coast of Africa into which my obstinate wickedness had plunged me; and who has been pleased to admit me to preach His glorious gospel." The last line of his will was that his funeral should be performed with as little expense, consistent with modest decency. He discouraged those people who wanted to have a monument erected to him, for in his mind he didn't feel that he was deserving of this honor.

We can acknowledge here today that the Lord has mercy and grace in pardoning whatever misfortunes there were in the past or are in the present or will be in the future. This great man died on December 21, 1807, at the age of eighty-two. The memories of his past may well give us the inspiration in realizing that the substance of our faith will not leave us desolate but will grow in abundance to signify that God's mercy, love, and grace know no bounds.

I would like to end with a prayer written by John Newton, in 1779, over two hundred years ago:

"May the grace of Christ our Savior and the Father's boundless love, with the Holy Spirit's favor rest upon them from above. Thus may they abide in union with each other and the Lord, and possess, in sweet communion, joys which Earth cannot afford."

Amen.

WHEN IN THE NIGHT THE HOMELESS HAD TO GO

I have a feeling about Ireland that haunts me. So I will write a villanelle that depicts the way the Irish suffered long ago. Their suffering was unconscionable, not just from the potato blight and the famine itself, but from the greedy and cruel policy that England dealt out to Ireland at the time.

John Mitchell, an Irish writer, deplores the famine (1846) as such: "The Irish watch the food melting in rottenness off the face of the earth while watching heavy-laden ships, freighted with yellow corn their own hands have sown and reaped, spreading sail for England."

When in the night the homeless had to go
In brutal times as stars turned gray and cold
For death came by with nothing more to
    show.

No more through Tara's Halls were sounds
    to blow;
Far, far from Erin's shores, though they were
    bold,
When in the night the homeless had to go.

They cursed the dark and reckoned with
    the foe,
But fortune in the fields diminished gold,
For death came by with nothing more to show.

The sharpest wounds of fate they dared
    to know,
Yet God was rich in pity to behold,
When in the night the homeless had to go.

They found another place where shamrocks
    grow;
Westward they sailed, creating new with old,
For death came by with nothing more to show.

They rose in glory, faith, with love to flow,
Laughed heartily and sang once tales were
    told;
When in the night the homeless had to go
For death came by with nothing more to show.

SPARE THE ROD AND SPOIL THE CHILD

In the forties my mother was nice to me, but if I talk back to her, she gives me a good tongue-banging or what we'd call "a severe knock." Before I leave for school, though, I make sure she has splits (kindling), and a full bucket of coal for our kitchen stove.

If I spill my porridge the first time, my mother can cope with that, yet if I spill it a second or third time, then she eyes me with that long-drawn-out stare and chides me, "Look! You're seven now and you don't have to spill anymore. So cut it out and don't do it again!" The usual response from my mother is: "DO AS YOU'RE TOLD!"

Another time, I take a crayon and scribble on a bedroom wall with all sorts of marks and weird scrawls that make no sense at all. Also, I use crayons for awhile till my mother stops me in my tracks. She takes them from me except for three of them that I chew and swallow for devilment in no time at all.

My mother spanks me once in awhile, especially when I pick a fight with someone just for the sake of doing it. One day my father was building an addition to our house when I hear him swearing. Evidently, he has hit his thumb and cries out, "Lord God, dying Jesus!" I am taken aback and rush into our kitchen and spurt out my father's selfsame words of invective. My mother is disgusted with me, "My law! Why are you swearing like that? What next?"

"Mom, I'm just repeating what Dad said when he hit himself with a hammer." If we boys are really bad or do something radically wrong, a typical mother can be heard saying, "Just you wait till your father comes home and he'll chastise you!"

If I misbehave and get in a bad way, my father takes me to my bedroom and spanks me with his huge hands that cover my backside quite adequately. He doesn't seem to have the heart to lay it on thick, for I believe he's aware of my sensitive nature. Occasionally, he may say, "Son, this is going to hurt me more than it's going to hurt you." As a result, his means of treatment towards me can be summed up in two words: "LOVE TAPS."

Most of the time, I'm a well behaved pupil and am fairly strait-laced, but in ninth grade I get in trouble every once in awhile. As a pupil in an academy, I give an example of what I can do with a little planning.

It is a cold winter's day and I decide to stay

in school during recess because my skates are being repaired. Outside the boys and girls are skating on the ice of our new rink while the darkening skies portend more snow for the next four days.

I'm in the classroom and begin to read the *Liberty* magazine, and I start to get bored. Then I gape at the inkwells on the desks and plainly succumb to my own idiocy even though my conscience alerts me about my foolishness.

Suddenly everything is pre-ordained in my mind. I pause momentarily, and then I fling myself into action, rush to the janitor's closet, pick up a galvanized bucket and methodically move from one aisle to another until I have poured every drop of ink into the bucket. I run with the contents and hide the bucket of ink in Mr. Spracklin's broom closet.

It strikes me that I will have to atone for my shenanigans. The school bell rings, and I begin to feel the intensity of the moment and sweat profusely. I realize I'm in for it, and I try to hide my hands in my pockets because the fingers are soiled with so much ink.

As the class begins, the pupils are ready to write with their pens and nibs, but there's no ink in their inkwells. I cannot keep a secret and admit to my guilt. The principal, Mr. Fred Rowe, is summoned to Mr. Andrews' classroom.

After many tormenting moments, I put up my hand and admit to my crime.

"Come up here, Hillier!" says the principal. With my head bowed in subservience, I wait to be questioned:

"What's going on here?"

"Nothing much, sir."

"What happened to the ink?"

"O! I left it in the janitor's closet?"

"I can't for the life of me understand why you would want to steal the ink."

"Sir, I have you know I never stole it!"

"You didn't?"

"No, sir! I just hid it in Mr. Spracklin's closet."

"Why did you do it, Hillier?"

"I'm not rightly sure, sir."

"You are not sure?"

"I daresay I am in a way, sir."

"Tell me: why did you take the ink?"

"For fun, sir!"

"Do you really believe something nonsensical like this can be for fun?"

"Not really, sir! I guess it's not so funny anymore."

"All right, Hillier, let us see how much fun this is going to be."

Mr. Rowe takes out his big black leather strap that lay hidden inconspicuously beneath his black gown.

"Hold out your hand!"

"Which one first, sir?"

"It doesn't matter!"

As soon as I extend my left hand, he begins his strapping. Instead of being angry with the principal, I feel he is doing exactly what I deserve. At any rate, I make those little grimaces when the strap lands on my palms. My lower lip curls up automatically.

When I keep putting out my hands, it seems that I have so many hands as if I will never run out of hands. One moment when Mr. Rowe is bringing the strap down on my right hand, I instinctively pull it away. Deep inside of me, I smirk as he receives the blow on the right side of his hip. The next time around, he gets more severe and straps me much harder.

My body shakes with emotion for it's like my hands are fluttering around in a gesture of imploring protest. I bite my lips and try to gain momentarily control of my shattered nerves. In retrospect, I wonder why I have to get into a terrible mess like this, for I have nothing against the school, nothing against the teachers, and nothing against the principal.

At last, just when my hands feel like heavy monstrous paws, the principal looks me squarely in the eye and tells me, "Let this be a lesson to you, Hillier. Now take your seat this instant!"

As I sit down, I don't know what to do with

my hands for they tingle with thousands and thousands of pins and needles pricking my skin and stinging like mad. I place the palms of my throbbing hands on the cool surface of my desk to salve my wounds.

When parents find their boys are being strapped, the parents give full approval of this form of discipline. In fact, they believe that sparing the rod does spoil the child. My parents, as much as they love me, believe in this form of discipline I have received by their remark: "SERVES YOU RIGHT!"

SUDDEN DEATH

As God is my Judge, know people die in the world, yet I never thought my sister, Helen, (Bobbie), would ever die. I never sought pity, but somehow I did look for justice to prevail when Bobbie was killed by a drunken driver on April 20, 1951, in Toronto, Ontario, Canada.

For sure I felt the fierce struggle in my tormented soul, for my sister was only twenty-two years old at the time. Our family was sitting down for tea in the early evening when we heard the shocking news on our Philco radio, without any prior notification of next of kin. We all cried out in utter disbelief, for we felt the news had betrayed the truth. The tears flowed automatically.

Then I wondered why this bizarre accident could have happened to my sister who had planned to come home to see us in springtime. There's not much consolation when death happens while we find ourselves left with our own hovering shadows. When a family is hit with such tragic news, there is not much left except the truth about the ugliness of death.

Then and there I thought, for sure, we can't take life for granted anymore. In March, 1951, Bobbie wrote me a letter saying how much she loved her work as a secretary with the Ontario Hydro Commission in Etobicoke. She also reminded me about my own life: "I know, George, you are doing very well in your running, and I am very proud of you. The only problem, so it seems, is that I hear you are not keeping up in your studies at Memorial College. I don't mean to tell you your business, but I would love for you to find a better balance between your running and your studies. Please keep in touch and I hope you can visit me when you come to run some races in Toronto next year. Good night for now. I am looking forward to going home for a well-deserved vacation in April. Love, from your sister, Bobbie."

I still have the article that appeared in the *Toronto Star* on April 20, 1951, when Bobbie was in a head-on crash that killed her instantly. The same news also appeared in *The Daily News* in St. John's, Newfoundland, on April 25, 1951. In death we have to truly know ourselves for what we are. When I first heard the news, I couldn't control myself, rose up from my chair at the kitchen table and went berserk. It seemed I was a hypocrite at a time when I should have brought more comfort and emotional support to my family.

I often yield to my fancies and suddenly kicked a baseboard and broke the big toe of my right foot. I didn't mind the pain and left the house to see my girlfriend, Olive, for commiseration and comfort in such frenzy. There was no sense in what I did and realized I should have told my parents where I was going. I apologized to them later for my drastic actions, and they forgave me for the overwhelming passion that seized me in my moment of hysteria.

Unfortunately, my feelings were strong and deeply rooted in my dilemma. Often, whenever bad things would happen in our family or anywhere, for that matter, my sisters used to say: "Above all, don't tell George!" Later on I began to resign myself to the facts of life with its good times and bad. So we can't always count on smooth sailing, clear skies, and tranquil waters.

Bobbie was waked in the front room of our home on McKay Street, and our house was filled with mourners. The thought of it all was the sorrow that we shared that was haunting then even as it still haunts us now. I suppose there's always something in life that we can never seem to understand in terms of its doubts and predicaments that may occur when you least expect it.

Nevertheless, we learned a hard lesson about Bobbie's death in our midst, and my parents, four sisters, my brother, and I continued in our lives with a deep sense of belonging that springs from our innermost being. The lesson we learned is that this tragedy made us stronger as we became more united as a family than ever before in our lives.

In retrospect, Bobbie, with all her niceties, was so pleasant and endearing in many ways with any nickels and dimes left over in her purse to serve my needs whenever I ran short. We got along well together, for she always took good care of her younger brother. I remember a time when she took me to Bowring Park so we could take a dip together, in the swimming pool. After a fresh swim, we walked together to the Bungalow where she treated me to a delicious Brookfield's orange-pineapple ice cream cone on a glorious summer's day in 1941. For sure, she was always faithful to any promises she made.

I dare say I shall never forget losing my sister since no words can fully express the sorrow I felt when my sad eyes fell on her beautiful face, so lonely there in her coffin. Out of a deep sense of nostalgia, when I was in Toronto for a race in 1953, I did take some time out to visit the scene of Bobbie's accident that occurred between the Thornhill and Langstaff stop lights on Yonge Street in Toronto.

Summarily, I have a moment to meditate: I still find that life is most precious. Sadly, though,

I have lost two sisters and a brother at this time. I have three beautiful sisters remaining, yet we all must adapt to our own trials in life with the knowledge that love, in the truest sense of the word, can never be lost, not even to death.

MY BROTHER,
THE SMOKER

Cigarettes killed my brother at the age of 44. He was a smoker who had those penetrating flashes of desire, even though his lungs were destroyed. By that time he had contracted a rare kind of cancer called "carcinoid syndrome." I am not sure, really, for the cancer may not have much of anything to do with the smoking. I know for sure John's smoking didn't help him any either.

Actually, this cancer had been in his system for many years, but once the symptoms of the disease appeared, it was too late to save him. He lived in agony his last four years. So did his family and friends. It was tragic to think that this handsome man, along with his personable ways and great ambitions for life, had to die so soon.

John was a successful civil engineer with a construction company in Toronto. He has two wonderful daughters, a healthy son, dedicated wife, and indeed everything to live for except the habit that changed his life forever.

When I last saw him in a Toronto hospital, he was heavily sedated, but he recognized me and lit up, so to speak. There he was with his Lucky Strike between his lips and the omnipresent ashtray perched upon a mound that was his enlarged stomach and distended liver.

With that down-to-earth comfort, he continued to draw his cigarette until the smoke had spun its gossamer threads through the air. What a way to relieve his anxiety and depression, but it was an unalterable fact; that was the only way he knew how to live.

One moment, when I thought his cigarette was going to touch upon the white sheet of his bed, I snatched it momentarily away from him. Then he knew something was missing in his life. He rose from his stupor and stared at me furiously. "My Jesus! Don't you take my cigarette away!" It was then that I thought of this old saying which goes something like this: "It's not so much the coughin' anymore, but the coffin they carry you off in." But smoking is not funny anymore. It never was.

One night when I stayed with him at the hospital, we talked about the old times, about everything. We even got to laugh at some funny things about life. He told me he hoped things would get better for him since he loved life and didn't want to end it.

I felt the sudden emptiness in my soul for my brother. No signs were positive since the surgeon told me John was terminal. Such emptiness simply indicated little time for a refill: a refill of joy, enthusiasm, or another cup of coffee.

It was in 1604, in Shakespeare's time, when King James I had his counterblast to smoking, "A custom loathsome to the eye, hateful to the nose, harmful to the braine, dangerous to the lungs, and in the black, stinking, fumes thereof, nearest resembling the horrible Stygian smoke of the pit that is bottomless."

I could never talk to my brother about quitting the smoking habit. He would listen, but not for long. Anyway, you cannot preach to a chronic smoker because he doesn't want to hear your sermon. For him, to quit cold turkey was impossible. He must have quit a thousand times. These were the times when he'd get nauseous and extremely nervous. The one time he quit was a miracle for John. He actually quit smoking for nine days and eight nights. Or was it eight days and nine nights? It took unusual determination to quit for that period of time. I once told John, "Just think of it now. This is your big chance. Don't blow it! You must quit—period! No butts about it."

John was tied up too much with the psychological craze and physiological need. There was no question about it; John was addicted. Everything he did was reinforced and perpetuated by the black, grimy tars and the narcotic effects of the drug, nicotine.

I still see my brother in that hospital bed sleeping and waiting for his wife, Suzanne, to visit him. I remember how troubled he looked, waking and waiting for the faded rag of a sky to burn into dawn. There was no happiness for him. John would be forgiven, but none of us would ever forget what happened here.

When I left my brother, I could sustain my tears no longer. There was that perfect and peculiar silence when the lips and heart are still. When I left him behind, I was crushed. I only wish that the dream I was dreaming didn't have to turn into a nightmare.

If you could see the faces in the hospital, perhaps you would not want to visit Marlboro Country. You would not be satisfied with the flavor there. The man who used to speak no longer has a voice. His larynx was cut out. The man in room 209 finds that a cigarette doesn't taste like a cigarette should. His tongue is gone. The patients here don't want to hear about the best selling tars or filter tips, or how they can escape into that splendid world with the mentholated taste.

If you are a smoker—light, medium, or heavy—take a trip to a hospital like the one I visited in Toronto. I believe you will find out for yourself how things are going in Marlboro Country. I don't think you will like it there.

MOTHER'S DAY IN THE NURSING HOME

When I saw her she wanted to say
things she never said before.
I tried to understand why she had
no more energy to spare.
She seemed to have so much to say
but could not speak. Then I tried my
best to make something out of nothing.
Anything was positive but most everything
I said came at best to nothing.
I helped her put her black shoes on.
The laces were stiff with the wild smell
of urine. She looked at me with spoils
of discontent upon her face. Her eyes
spoke to me: "I am the victim
of some undisputed prey."
She is not aware of what has been
and starts off once more into her room
so she can penetrate the darkness.
I tell her about the rhythm of walking
in the sun. We walk together in painful
communion of two hearts in one. There
is a frail structure to my imaginings
for she has lost her symmetry.
She alters her pace and has the nerve

to stop. She is as terrified as a deer frozen in its tracks—waiting in nakedness for any sudden subtle move. If she falls she may not rise again. The sun is now too abrupt, too wild and rigorous for the light interrupts her serenity. I take her back to her room and say goodbye. As I leave her, she pauses, glances back at me and walks away secretly. That last look made me desperate and forlorn for my heart choked with passion, but I walked away mighty proud of a mother whose love was always
her constant duty.

MY DAD:
THE LAST GOODBYE

I said goodbye to my father at the airport. Well, I tried anyway. "Dad, I will see you next summer. Take care of yourself and Mom." Instead, I wanted to say, "Dad, I love you, my real friend." As we drove along, my father said, "Son, I just want you to know if you come back next summer, I might not be here."

"O, Dad! Please don't say that now!" We shook hands, and when I turned around and walked toward the plane, I wanted to look back again, but I never did for the heart had already stretched to its limitations. He was right. He died in the fall of the year.

Thank you, Dad, for stoking the furnace on those freezing winter nights; for all your carpentry work in building so much furniture for others; for telling me I'd see God in a nobler way in Sunday school. Thank you for your echoes of love, for your comfort when I thought shadows were gray ghosts chasing me everywhere in the longest nights of every arctic summer, for all the fine trouting times we had together when you always brought home the bacon. Thank you for your winter's protection while I was blindly going through my maze of dead-ends as a student, for all your precious clowning, for all the times you said, "Lord save us!" that saved us every time, for the intimate magic in being blind as a bat to all my faults, for your buoyancy at Christmas dinner when you'd say, "This sure calls for a celebration!"

Now time is merely predatory and though I see, I no longer see clearly beyond since the present still has yesterday's soulful look about it when I recall our wild heroics and sweet liaisons.

BIBLE LESSONS I LEARNED FROM JESSIE CAROLINE WILCOX CASSIDY

I learned from my great-grandmother everything I wanted to know about God. I read the Bible as much as I could, but that does not mean I understood everything. I could not see God as much as I strained my eyes, and even when I went to the toilet at Wesley United Church, I had a hunch God was right behind me. By reading the Bible I got my own picture of Him, and to me, anyway, He was dark in complexion. I surmised that, "How can you be a pale face in the sun's heat of Palestine and Jerusalem and other places in the Middle East and not be tanned?"

Then I thought if we didn't receive what God has promised us, then we had better look to our side of the covenant, for I dare say the fault cannot be blamed on God. For it is written in God's unmistaken words that He will not do you in: "For the Lord God is a sun and shield: the Lord will give grace and glory; no good thing will He withhold from them that walk uprightly (Psalm 84:11).

So we learn that there's no conflict to God's covenant when we believe in what he says. All we have to do is to walk uprightly in order to follow in His footsteps. This doing just what it means we should be doing in His name, indeed, will put more hope and joy in our hearts.

Many years later I began to read about Saint Augustine. I found the *Confessions of St. Augustine* exciting but also overwhelming. Imagine reading about a holy man who lived over 1600 years ago. This great man tells us how he had to go in search of God while he is still being caught up in idleness and neglect of his studies. Indeed, it took St. Augustine a long time to get rid of his old habits. Yet I find from his confessions that he found a way in believing that Jesus Christ lives in all of our hearts. He realized he was far from being perfect, but he found there's no excuse to uphold a standard that is less than perfect. Moreover, no matter what St. Augustine did, he did in the name of God Almighty by assisting others to find that Christ is their Savior and Lord. In order to affect a change in sinners, he taught them to forget their own selfish desires; instead, they must learn that God's message on earth is planned, " 'not by might, nor by power, but by My spirit,' saith the Lord of Hosts." (Zechariah 4:6).

I find when I begin to read about this saint's

confessions that I receive magnanimous comfort as a Christian that we have such a dedicated man who came on earth to spread God's Holy Word and Gospel.

It is both inspirational and heart-rending when I sit down and learn about St. Augustine's Christian philosophy. As an example, I would like to characterize his quintessential wisdom by referring to one passage in his text to emphasize this great man's faith and true humility:

"I acknowledge Thee, Lord of Heaven and Earth, and praise Thee for my first rudiments of being, and my infancy, whereof I remember nothing; for Thou hast appointed that man should from others guess much as to himself; and believe much on the strength of weak females. Even then I had being and life, and (at my infancy's close) I could seek for signs whereby to make known to others my sensations. Whence could such a being be, save from Thee, Lord, in whom essence and life are one? For Thou Thyself art supremely Essence and Life. "For Thou art most high, and art not changed," (Malachi 3:6) neither in Thee doth today come to a close; yet in Thee doth it come to a close; because all such things also are in Thee. For they had no way to pass away, unless Thou upheldest them. And since, Thy years fail not. Thy years are one today. How many of ours and our father's years have flowed away through Thy "today," and from it received the measure and the mould of such being as they had; and still others shall flow away, and so receive the mould of their degree of being. But "Thou art still the same," (Psalm 102:27) and all things tomorrow, and all beyond, and all of yesterday, and all behind it, Thou hast done today. What is it to let me, though any comprehend not this? Let him also rejoice and say, "What thing is this?" (Exodus 16:15) Let him rejoice even thus; and be content rather by not discovering to discover Thee, than by discovering not to discover Thee."

NEWFOUNDLAND

As a daughter to mother England, Newfoundland retained its spirit of monarchy and still slept in the womb of the century, by frankly admitting with pride of birth that Newfoundland, after all, is Britain's oldest colony. At a moment's notice, when any war came, the island straightened up as soldiers would go to the sound of distant bugles. Anytime bugles sounded the strains of war, the island responded with its good-natured provincial fate.

When I was twelve, I used to hear the city of St. John's speak the language of war. Patriotism raced through the city like a hurricane. I felt going off to war was the gesture of obedient listening, and the call of the spirit to struggle against the evils of the world.

Since I was too young to fight, it was my solemn duty to quiver with resentment against the likes of those who failed in their duty at a critical period in an island's life. Everyone who was eligible to go had to go as far as I was concerned. What is more consoling, more tender, than a man who is willing to sacrifice his life for God, King, and Country? I was, too, concerned about the slacker. In my curious make-up, I felt no one has any use for a coward during a crisis. Don't you understand me? Heroes are the style. Never slackers.

In school we had to memorize and recite a prayer taken from Admiral Nelson's own diary, "May the great God, whom I worship, grant to my country, and for the benefit of Europe in general, a great and glorious victory, and may no misconduct in anyone tarnish it, and may humanity after the victory be the predominant feature in the British Fleet." I must have pored over that message a thousand times till I learned it by heart. This kind of sentiment promoted the righteousness of a cause among us school children.

I felt Sunday was different because the air was different from any other days of the week, that is, because I swear that Sunday carried the distinct aroma of God's almighty presence. I watched the cruel wind whip sheets of snow and sleet from the flat roofs of the colorfully, squared houses onward to the street.

On my way to Sunday school one rainy afternoon, I tried my best to become a true believer, and actually gathered up enough courage to ask God, "Please, God, for heaven's sake, make them stop the war. Make them stop the killings. You're the only one able enough to stop the war. Remember my prayer. Amen."

I'd sit with suspended breath and half-closed

eyes, and peal forth my desires and common sense. Once in a while, especially if something or other were bothering me, I would add to my little prayer, ". . . or else I will never forgive you. I'm sure you know just what I mean by that. That's all. Amen." On my way home I blinked my eyes, and felt the ice crystals clinging to my eyelashes, and listened to the variety of the wind's voices that carried the storm down from the north. Unfortunately, this was not the day to make snowballs.

I thought for sure when the sun came out the next morning, that God in His inimitable way had answered my prayer, in part at least. A beginning was a beginning, even if it resulted in a fragment of a reply. Anyway it was better than no response at all. I started to think that if God could make the world in six days, then He could in all assurance stop the war in one. Make no mistake about it, though, the sun was God's bright candle.

God was the invisible man who was everywhere and nowhere at the same time. To me at times He was the arrogant one who must have lost His passionate energy for youth and its desires. Then my mind wondered how prayers could be possibly answered or how could blessings open my eyes to peace in credible ways. I hoped that I would have gotten some answer by now. Then I'd reflect upon

1 Corinthians 2:9, "What no eye has seen, nor ear heard, nor the heart of man conceived, what God has prepared for those who love Him." Most of the time, I had to have faith in myself. Let God be God and man be man. Man would stay the same. He would be like the politician. He would never reform. He would merely change his vice. There was no question in my mind that a man held his gifts in fief from the devil, and not from Almighty God. And come to think of it, it was wonderful believing in dreams, and in believing in them as one believes in the soul's salvation. If the character of my belief would change, I would continue to believe in myself or in my mother or in my father whose footsteps I would gladly follow.

Trying to find out more about a God for being got to be a scary business. I mean there was all that deadly waiting, if you know what I mean. I asked myself, "What if God actually came to me in a blaze of glory as promised?" I would, no doubt, be visibly shocked by His presence, or probably die outright from the revelation. I still have a characteristic habit of glancing over my shoulder in order to prepare for any sudden emergency.

I went to Wesley Sunday School not so much that I always wanted to go, but because as my father put it, "It will do you the world of good, that is, if you want God to be on your side." One time I asked my father, "Dad, how come you never go to church?" And he replied, "That's easy, son! I've already been." He was in church once upon a time, the only time, and that was when he married my mother. My mother assured me that church would help to civilize me. "The experience will give you a lift. Everyone needs a freshening of the spirit once in a while."

It was not so easy concentrating on the images from Jeremiah. Yet I was the number one, the gullible one. I took everything hook, line, and sinker. My mind was more like my mother's colander, but my restless eyes, were, indeed, full of visions. I could feel the excitement rise up in me as I bowed in prayer. Suddenly, in my conscience, I had a swift vision of a bearded man lying down somewhere on a desert sand. Was he the one I was perhaps looking for? It is hard to imagine how I was supposed to believe. I tried to conjure up the proper images during a prayer, swallowed my Beechnut gum, instead of hiding it under a chair, and was waiting for my teacher to tell me about the prodigal son. The collection was taken up, and there we were with our peace offerings and ingratiating smiles, for I was well aware of the copper burning a hole in my pocket. The song we sang went like this,

"Dropping, dropping, dropping, dropping,
hear those pennies fall, everyone for Jesus,
He will bless them all."

There I was, actually believing that God would come around later to pick up His just rewards. You see, I was that extraordinary Methodist going about my madness. Perhaps if I were to doubt God, then I was afraid I might summarily die for my mortal sins. Then if I were to believe in Him, I thought for sure I'd be swept unconsciously away in His surging tide. My impressions came first; left me, came back, and flashed in and out of my mind while I was in church. I took everything I learned to heart. Once I got outside the church, I could breathe a sigh of relief.

As soon as I returned home, I'd go to my room where it was quiet. Undisturbed, I tried to get my mind away from God and the problems of His hysterical world. Things that meant so much to me years ago have lost some of their meaning. A young believer is the only true believer in my book. Of course, if God shrieks above a ragged edge of a mountain, while the sun is making the ice shine on the spurs below, and He removes all doubts away, then will I raise myself and accept the finger of Providence pointing. Often would I look inwardly, argue with myself, and then talk with someone who would bully me into courage, so I'd have some kind of substitute for a missing God.

Downtown I would hear women gossiping in front of shops about the Second World War and any kind of trivial matters and, at the same time, hear the clopping of horses' hooves upon gray cobblestones of Water Street. On my street I would see mothers bring out their baskets of wrung out clothes and hang them out on the lines in the back yards to dry in the October sun. Mrs. Percy adjusts the pole so the damp clothes will hang higher in the fresh breezes. She takes a clothespin out of her mouth and speaks over the picket fence to her neighbor, Mrs. Delaney.

Mrs. Percy is happy, "Well, I heard from Gerald yesterday. He's in France. That much I know. It was only a short letter. He is dying for smokes. He misses his Royal Blends. He appears to be in good fettle. You know how it is with boys, Clara. They never tell you what they really think. Only what you wish to hear."

Mrs. Delaney, who is much older than Mrs. Percy, and childless, responds, "I know Gerald. He'll do fine. I must get together a little package and send it off to him in a few days. I will send him some cigarettes, too. You know I pray for Gerald every day, and I will continue to do so until he returns from overseas, God willing."

Mrs. Percy continues on, "Did you know the two Thompson boys joined up in the Royal Navy two days ago? I never thought it would happen, knowing poor Sara. She is beside herself." I used to wonder what it was within a woman whose son went into battle. What lie hidden beneath the exterior of her being, that had awakened the strange feeling of possession called motherhood? Before Mrs. Percy goes into her basement with her basket, Mrs. Delaney says to her, "Yes, I know, my dear, Sara is in a bad way. I'm sure you know where to turn for help. Sara will get over the shock of it. It will take time, all right. What else is there except to put up a good fight? Her boys will have to do the very same thing. That's for sure." I noticed the mothers would be nervous when the mailman came by, hoping for a letter, yet apprehensive about what they will know, and hoping that the news will not shatter their nerves.

Mrs. Thompson was aware of the enormity of the war since she had two uncles who went across in the First Five Hundred. No one seems to want to live war again, unless, of course, you have to live it over again. What can you do about it anyway? It's been that way since Neanderthal or the age of tooth and claw.

When it came time to figuring out what the war was all about, often there was no verbal response to a son's goodbye except faces of mothers, fathers, sisters, and brothers left empty and stupefied.

A family left alone in tormenting doubt often has to call upon heaven as witness since such a task is beyond the power of mortal man. Above all, if I were to think of some kind of remedy to the war, I would open up a Society for the Prevention of Cruelty to Mothers.

Freedom was the ultimate objective in war— freedom from the Germans, and freedom from the terror of someone knocking on your door at night. For all those who enlisted, the news was received with nods of approval and heads bowed in prayer. The war would lie on the world's body like a bloody nightmare.

What a day it was for the Newfoundlanders, the numberless numbers, who fought at Beaumont Hamel, suffered in rank and file, regimented up to their very death, up to the grave, into which they were shoved to the accompaniment of salvos from the mouths of German cannons. The sound of taps never dies away. One summer, when clouds and shadows of clouds raced across the sky, I heard the piercing cries from seagulls, walked like a soldier, swung my arms like a soldier, breathed the air freely, and prepared to have an enjoyable day. I could hear the train coming out of the station, click, clacking its way to Port Aux

Basques, with wheels finding their way on narrow-gauged tracks. The train's whistle emitted a mournful sound till I could hear the sound no more.

On my way to Victoria Park, I looked inside the fleur de lis spears of a green iron fence, and observed three old First World War veterans chewing the rag. I'm sure they were talking about the good times and the bad.

These veterans were sitting on a wooden bench, and spoke about anything in general, but they laughed and laughed about the war. They looked like schoolboys who were discussing the misery of examinations they had just gone through. Far better than lingering at the Poor House on Sudbury Street. When it was time for them to go, I noticed three of them hobbling toward the exit. However, they had only three legs and six rattling crutches among them. On the right went one man whose right leg had been saved. On the left went his counterpart, hopping on his left leg. In the middle was the poor angishore, the left-over of a human body, with his lower jaw missing and his left leg gone, swinging between the high crutches. It was, no doubt, my idea of a living picture of ghosts. Their empty trousers were raised by safety pins up to their chests. I am bloody certain if God had seen them, He would have cried out in pain. What a poet's eye for symmetry. You see, their crutches were precious objects confided to their care. I was lost for a moment in my thoughts. It was hard to simulate their happiness. That night when I went to sleep, I took the nightmare with me.

Everybody in the city waits eagerly to honor the hero. It is something intangible, which cannot be expressed in words, but which, nevertheless, enriches the lives of everyone who sleeps safely at night. I'm sure mothers would have been ashamed to stand there without a hero for a son. After all, I suppose, God didn't turn water into wine for nothing.

I lived beside a river in the cup-shaped valley. The river, in all its moods and changes, swept through the valley from the springs of its far-away origins to the ocean of its final endeavor. I was at peace with the river, but at war with the world. On Memorial Day, I would look at the old veterans with worn medals on their frayed lapels. I had compassion for the hero and only disdain for the slacker. How can slackers forget the glory of their heritage? I studied them with my cold, suspicious eyes. Don't they realize that patriotism is based upon the verities of mankind?

Who was my hero? Why, none other than the Fighting Newfoundlander, the classic statue at Bowring park, just west of the city. Now there is a man symbolic of the genuine fighter ready to hurl a hand grenade. Sentimentally, that was one reason enough for walking to the park. I would look for a long time at that body and at that face and, invariably, get the goose bumps by the majesty of its emotions. The statue was so vivid among the flowers and the trees beside the Bungalow. Nostalgia always lures me back. I know now that the statue itself is representative of all those Newfoundlanders who fought in the wars: in the Navy, the Army, the Air Force, and the Merchant Marine.

My living hero ran a drug store at the corner of Water Street and Job. His name was Tommy Ricketts. Usually our family dealt with Edwards the Druggist because it was near home. Yet I convinced my mother that going to Ricketts was worth the trip, though it was about a mile longer. It didn't matter. I was going to meet the hero. When I first laid eyes on this man, I was in awe of him, whether he knew it or not. I gave him my prescription, and he took it with a minimum of words. I expected more from him. Instead of having a hero's face, or the type I had envisioned, his expression was a nasty one. I, for sure, was taken by surprise. To me he had a worried look as if he had been guilty for something he had done, one way or another.

For the life of me, I could never figure it out. I was flustered emotionally; a frog was caught in my throat. It made me inarticulate because my tongue got stuck and my lips were made of stone. I tried my best by squeaking out some respectable words, "Sir, you were some great in the war!" Again I was rebuffed. He completely ignored what I said to him so strenuously. There was no response except a slight twitch he made with the tidy moustache tucked beneath his nostrils. He could only remain his shy, evasive self. I was considerably impressed with an account of his exploits as a seventeen year old in the heat of battle in France. This is an excerpt from the *London Gazette* of January 6, 1919:

"Private Ricketts at once volunteered to go forward with his section commander and a Lewis gun to attempt to outflank the battery. Advancing by short rushes under heavy fire from enemy machine guns with the hostile battery, their ammunition was exhausted when still 300 yards from the battery.

The enemy, seeing an opportunity to get their field guns away, began to bring up gun teams. Private Ricketts, at once realizing the situation, doubled back 100 yards under the heaviest machine gun fire, procured further ammunition, and dashed back again to the Lewis gun, and by very accurate fire drove the enemy and the gun teams into a farm.

His platoon then advanced without casualties

and captured the four field guns, four machine guns, and eight prisoners. A fifth field gun was subsequently intercepted by fire and captured.

By his presence of mind in anticipating the enemy intention and his utter disregard of personal safety, Private Ricketts secured the further supply of ammunition which directly resulted in these important captures and undoubtedly saved many lives."

In retrospect, I may have discovered a little something about this man's tragic loneliness that may have reached the point of satiety. Tommy Ricketts was the youngest winner of the Victoria Cross in the British Army. The man remained his solid self by shunning the press, radio, and television. In other words, he avoided the fanfare and was resolute in his convictions till the day he died on February 10, 1967.

I always thought I had a fairly decent nature. Yet I had room enough to make exceptions for slackers. I used to say, "May God in his eternal wisdom preserve us from the slackers whose consciences let them sleep at night." There was some way I had to pull my weight, all 87 pounds of me. Anyone I saw on the street on my way to school who looked eligible to fight, but was reluctant, I would get my licks in, by calling out stridently, "Slacker! Slacker! Slacker!"

On the one hand, I would see Newfoundlanders with the essence of old saints and martyrs, living poorly, but living happily; sympathetic mortals, slowly sacrificing themselves in war, and willing to wreck everything except their hopes and dreams for a cause they believed was right. On the other hand, I would see slackers and ask myself, "Why should they receive a special dispensation not to have to go to war?" Respect for the slacker counted for nothing in my mind.

Then, later on, when I got older, I started to wonder if my heart was really embedded in the rock of patriotism. I started to question whether or not I would be willing to go to war and prepare for my own death. In the drama of it all, though victory would be a cherished cause, it is still one man's life balanced against the risk of death. I began gradually to believe that not everyone could expect to be bold warriors. I'm sure the slackers who came home from their work would breathe more contentedly knowing I would not be present to hurl my jingoistic insults at them. I always remember one mother who shook with emotion. I saw her hands raised in a gesture of imploring protest against the war. She was filled with dark shadows of memories that came into her blue eyes. She was the one who told her friends in no uncertain terms, "I will not send my son into a war spawned by the devil. I know man is the terror. He is the creator of war and war is hell. There is no way I will choose hell for my son."

Finally, I asked myself another question, "Since you would never snare rabbits or shoot partridge, would you, as a result, go into a war and deliberately kill a man in cold blood?" It was at that precise moment, when I realized how hard it must be for a man to turn into a bloodthirsty militarist. I thought about the poor devils in the war who had no secrets left. Somehow it doesn't take too long to be demoralized by man's desire for oblivion. I began to sympathize with the mother who was aghast about the brutality of war. She was deadly opposed to justifiable slaughter. It is impossible to predict the exact moment at which the worm will turn and the human heart revolt.

BAULINE

Here in St. John's the rain comes only when
You expect it. You expect it. In Bauline,
After a roller-coaster ride in sister Libby's
      car,
We notice the sun comes out more willingly.
And when the sun comes out, isn't this
      creation
Filled with glory? Isn't this the light of it?
The all-sufficient love of it?

At the Glover home where ghosts of Kings
      reside,
Bob and Bertie Glover, George and Midge
      Faulkner,
Sister Libby Hogan, her daughter, Andrea,
And I eat and drink and sing in order of
      merriment.
Make a new kind of picture and you paint
A new kind of life in Bauline where the rest
Of the world stays in exile.

A house is a house and windows are eyes.
Eyes look out to the ocean. Eyes stare at
The fish-starved sea where fragile fishermen
Wait for tenured cod and a lifetime
      guarantee.

Let expressions come, but not in
Shallowed breaths.

Together we're quick off the mark. We sing
Energetically. We buoy up our tuneful
Voices. Even when we miss some of the
    words,
We never miss the mood of songs. George
    Faulkner
(Let 'er rip and jump for joy!) played the
    guitar
While Bertie played her spoons. Our voices
    went on
And on, but never ad nauseam.

Bauline is the long-looked-for revelation:
Last green of summer, first gold of fall.
Atmospheric. Oceanic. Touching. Exalted
    mountains
And low-lying hills. I don't forget the
    extraordinary
Air, clean and clear.

We recycle the past with anthology of song
To make the mood of the moment
Much more memorable. Let me see: what
    about
"Red River River Valley" next time or
"Kelligrew's Soiree?"

When the night is over, we respond
To the blessed silence with a silence
Of our own. In the darkness of the night,
Stars uphold the sky. There are too many
To fill the eyes. How many are enough?

We are now in our own different corners. Yet
We are still present, superbly anecdotal,
    like in a
Fleshed-out play, convincingly Arthurian,
    reminiscing
And waiting for the sequel to begin.

NO MAN IS AN ISLAND, ALMOST

A great silence fell on St. John's when we heard the news of Herb Chafe's death at the age of 21. Early in the morning of July 18, 1952, Herb was in a jeep going much too fast on a slippery, fog-enshrouded highway. The jeep skidded and crashed off the road and overturned near Dunne's Lane on Topsail Road. The driver failed to make a sharp curve and swung into a ditch.

A skull fracture was the cause of Herb's death. His friends, Alistair Graham and Colin Taylor, were released from hospital after treatment for minor injuries.

That spring, Herb had been commissioned as a second lieutenant after three years in the COTC (the Canadian Officers' Training Corps) at Memorial University and the Nova Scotia Technical College. Herb was about to enter his final year for a civil engineering degree, and was planning to enter the active force as a career.

Those of us who remember Herb—and we are legion—realize things about life and death the same way we learn how much easier it is to say hello than to say goodbye. Of course, we like the idea that we may be lifted out of darkness into light, out of sorrow into peace, and out of a spirit of heaviness into a spirit of hope.

Our collection of Herb's memories defines us. Believe it or not, we may think in a sense that Herb Chafe never died because we carried him with us over the long haul. He was our alter ego, our second self. What about the torch he left behind? Oh, we carried it and kept on going.

Many people live their lives to satisfy themselves, but Herb was not one of them. He was dedicated to his family, his friends, and was one of the kindest men you would ever wish to meet.

They say no man is an island, but let me tell you, Herb Chafe was.

Albert Burgess and Herb were good friends from Grade 7 up to first year at college. After one year, Albert decided to leave and go to sea to make his living.

He reminisces, "Herb and I enjoyed the winter best because we loved cross-country skiing. We'd ski wherever there was a patch of snow. We used to walk long distances to ski behind Herb's aunt's house on Topsail Road.

"Skiing was a tremendous challenge for us and we would ski for hours around Virginia Waters until it got dark. One Saturday night we were coming home around 10 and we were walking on the road with the moon and stars and we sang 'Cool, cool water' to the top of our lungs. Herb sure could harmonize.

"Herb was in excellent condition and as a result he was first in everything, even if it were a three-legged race or tiddlywinks. Whatever activity, there was Herb with his great competitive spirit.

"He excelled in sports, but he never flaunted his abilities. In class he was the top student, but he always took time out to help us lesser mortals in any school subject. There was a wonderful spirit about him no matter what the circumstances. I suppose it was all part of his wholesome personality.

"We used to have the "House" system in school. Herb played soccer for MacPherson House while I played for Harrington. One time Herb was scrambling for the ball and gave me a body check I never forgot. I thought I was hit by a Mack truck. I loved being on Herb's team for it was less hazardous to my health.

"I can see him now on our way to a movie at the Nickel Theatre, wearing his red flannel shirt and his snazzy camel-hair sports jacket. I know for sure when Herb died I lost the best friend I ever had."

I think of 1948 and the years that followed. I see Herb Chafe as he sits on an old, black, shiny leather couch in the Common Room at Memorial College on Parade Street. He leans his head back against a yellow, glossy-painted wall, stretches out his long legs and then crosses them.

A pipe is wedged in the right corner of his mouth and he becomes the classic picture of contentment. His sky-blue eyes are focused on a text he is studying for some exam in an engineering class with Professor Stan Carew.

While he is soaring to great academic heights, I am busy majoring in running with a minor in ping pong. Above all, Herb is now, no less, the President of the Students' Representative Council. I am impressed with his creativity and his astuteness in settling student matters.

One afternoon, the term grades are posted on a wall. He looks up at his score. He is on top in chemistry with 97 per cent. I am amazed that anyone can manage to receive such a high numerical grade.

It's strange, in a way, because it appears to have come as no surprise to him at all. The bad news is I got a 42 per cent. The good news, however, is that 40 was a passing grade way back then.

Along with Herb's academic distinction, he was also excellent in sports. I am not his friend; instead, he is my absolute hero. I recall walking to Memorial College one morning.

I am privileged to wait for him as he emerges from his home on Cabot Street. As we walk together along LeMarchant Road, step-for-step, my two steps to his gigantic one, I can tell you that modesty is written all over his handsome face. He is wearing a red flannel shirt.

Suddenly, though, the day is dark and the night turns black. I learn that Herb Chafe has died. I am beside myself. It is incredible that a man so young can die before the world in such a tragic way as this. To all appearances it's like hope is lost and good is defeated.

Years later, I arrived in Toronto for a marathon run. Somehow, I got the notion to search in many stores to find something that resembles the shirt Herb used to wear.

I could not help myself; I was his righteous follower. Although I never smoked, I decided for old times' sake to buy a pipe and some Prince Albert tobacco. As I began to puff, I coughed and gasped for breath, yet I smelled the sweet, delicious clouds of smoke. I only lasted for a few days, and came to find I am strongly allergic to tobacco.

In retrospect I am inspired by the life of this man, just as I believe a dream will bring greater promise for tomorrow.

WAITING FOR YOU IN COUNTY CLARE, IRELAND

When you first see Ireland, you watch the dawn lift darkness from the earth like a new world breaking in glory around you. The feeling is awe; awe from the intensity of its immobile face, reflecting days gone by; how far gone by, too, they must have been.

Janemarie and you drive from Shannon Airport in a rented car. You're a creature of habit and must adapt to driving on the wrong side of the road. You mutually agree that you will make no mistakes, that is, until, you get lost in Lisdoonvarna, twice found yourselves in Ennistymon, on your route to Doolin way down in County Clare.

You are in Doolin now and you hear birds sing. Rivers wait for their salmon. You witness O'Donoghue's cows getting their feed from farmer Pat whose toil is holy prayer. You know all about "Patty's Lament," the fear and the lust of the English facing the Irish on every side.

You learn about the tangles, lost shapes and straying cries. As you stand in West Clare, you see where the English destroyed the cottages of the Irish who, as a result of the potato blight, were unable to keep up their monthly payments. (The human condition was explained to you years ago by a Beefeater before you entered the Tower of London, "I must tell you when it came to cruelty, the English were most proficient.")

The somber green tranquility seeps into your very being. Janemarie finds there's nothing better than a good book along with the contentment of a peat fire on a cold, unrelenting night.

Doolin, with its sense of pride, tries to keep up with the times. You look through your windshield and notice a bumper sticker, no doubt, a current message about our self-preservation: "Horn Broke! Look For Finger!"

You meet a man who is a friend, Big Liam McCauley, who sighs benevolently while remembering his 86 years. In a providential way shadows come and go while his day seems as if it rises to shed its light on everything.

Every breath he takes carries its own echo of confirmation. Liam remembers when he languished as a poet:

"You are not old when your hair turns gray.
You are not old when your teeth decay,
But when your head makes a date
That your body can't keep,

Then you're heading, brother,
For that long, last sleep."

Big Liam moves slowly but persistently so the day doesn't start unexpectedly without him. He walks a bit every day and memorizes the rain and fog. He knows how the weather goes.

"It only rained twice last week," he says, "the first time for three days and the second time for four."

The sun, however, is shining as we follow a path to Galway Bay. You watch him as he sizes up a flotilla of boats and the womby roundness of the bay.

Liam complains that he is "galled by the gulls of Galway" as he winks at you facetiously, and summarily breaks up the multitude of wrinkles on his swarthy face.

As we walk together, the moods compound in the exhausted silence. Liam walks a little, stops a little, and then continues on his giddy ritual till he gets to his place where laburnum tendrils trail.

Having been bent by the burden of so many winters, he still relishes the rapture of going home, even though his wife is gone. He is grateful for the magic motives of a day. It is time to say goodbye.

Yet, just as you say goodbye, you suspect Big Liam's sacred wish is not to be left alone.

Out of the fog, out of the dim beginning of things, out of the shifting shadows, emerges the composed, light-stepping figure of a shepherd, eminently serene in the small-high mightiness of the pastoral scene. You come to an abrupt stop in front of a small bridge and roll down your window and say,

"I'm sorry, sir! I almost knocked over one of your lambs!"

"Not a'tall, not a'tall! 'Tis foolery! I have a hundred and t'irty nine left!"

You find everything remarkable. His face wears a sad beauty of its own and his black hair and bushy eyebrows show up perfectly against his bright, sunny skin. His eyes sparkle with a laugh latent in them. In fact, you are deeply moved by the peculiar light that plays over his countenance on a day in Doolin where spite dies hard.

"Will ye come in for a cup of tea?" These are the words coming from a woman who owns a dry goods store in Galway.

"Yes! Yes! Thank you for your kindness."

"Don't mention it!"

"O, my!" You say to her, "This is like being home."

"O! Where is that?"

"In St. John's, Newfoundland!"

" 'Tis a small world, isn't it? I know some relatives who live there."

We talk on and on, and then she passes me a scone and I'm eating and drinking with delight. When the going gets tough, Janemarie goes shopping and is in the process of buying three pure handknit sweaters in the Republic of Ireland by Inisfree.

The lady is most cordial, but later on she confides in you as her eyes are turned to nature, "You see my son, Desmond, with your wife over there?"

"Yes!"

"Two years ago he was doing quite well in medical school, but last winter he got into a car accident and has never been the same since. About all Desmond can do now is sell goods in my store."

Suddenly, I am devastated by hearing such tragic news. Your heart cries out to her: "I am so sorry that this has happened. You must be brave."

"O! I take it all in stride. I have to be upbeat and learn to endure the pain. If I didn't have my faith, I don't know what I'd do. Every morning I get up, I have to say to myself, 'This is the day which the Lord has made. Let us rejoice in it.'"

You get used to the smirr (drizzling rain) and you walk through the decorated and clustered, arched doorways. If you're six feet tall or more you may have to lower your halo.

You do or else you may end up with a pre-frontal lobotomy by the time you pass through.

As the westerly wind blows in, you are in sight of the Cliffs of Moher. They stretch along the coast of Clare and probably reach up to 600 feet or more. The cliffs remind you of a huge curtain in a scene from a Shakespearean tragedy.

You still hear the stories about Ireland—about the conquered and the conqueror. You come to hear the tenors singing in the Irish pubs all the time.

Yet Doolin is the same as anywhere just as long as the sun and the earth learn how it is to juxtapose. So Ireland is what it is supposed to be: sweet in every form to rouse a corresponding echo in the soul of everyone.

But the holiday is over. You run short of panegyrics now. And what about the world? Will it still be waiting for you in Doolin, way down in County Clare?

UNCLE SAM

Beyond the pale of passing years,
Sam Wilson won enduring fame;
this symbol born in Arlington
enhances freedom with his name.

We now salute our Uncle Sam
who still preserves our liberty,
for glory with its touch of pride
is etched in landscape's memory.

The hope and trust we put in God,
impulses of a heartfelt prayer,
when they who fought in history
kept up the faith without the fear.

In life's victory and defeat,
to face the challenge, it may seem,
though human pride and valor rise,
the best we have is what we dream.

A glorious tribute to our days,
for love enduring, seeking grace,
we rise above adversity,
sustaining hope to keep the peace.

PANSY

When our sons, George and David, were nine and five years old, the boys wanted to have a cat as a pet. Unfortunately, I was allergic to cat fur. I was, however, outvoted three to one when a family vote was taken.

Our friends, the Ware family, had just had a new batch of kittens. Fortunately, we were given "the pick of the litter." We chose a calico money cat immediately and named her Pansy because of her colors and her face that resembled the pansy flower.

Right from the start Pansy became an important member of the Hillier family. As a kitten she wallowed in our attention. She was playful, friendly, and lovable. She was a favorite of the students who came daily to our private reading clinic and quickly became the official greeter who welcomed the students. In turn, she expected to receive a gentle stroking of her back as her reward.

During the end of her first year, Pansy became pregnant. We thought this would be an ideal opportunity for our sons to learn about the birth process. Naturally, Pansy was nurtured and pampered with the best nutrition and a visit to our veterinarian.

I built a special birthing crib in anticipation of her delivery. Early one Saturday morning in springtime, Pansy awakened me by pouncing on my stomach while I slept. I alerted the boys and Janemarie what was about to occur.

I held Pansy gently and placed her into her crib. Shortly she settled down. My son, George, and my wife, got scared and left the room temporarily. David, however, sat watching the action and there was plenty of action.

I helped to deliver the first kitten with a little coaxing and watched as five more kittens emerged before our very eyes in timely fashion. I thought the delivery was complete after six kittens emerged safely. Then I looked at Pansy's face with her eyes wide open, and she didn't seem completely content. Soon I noticed there was another kitten struggling to come out. I gently helped Pansy with the delivery of Sport, a gray and white tiger. Undoubtedly, Sport, after all the ructions going on, was the last of the litter. Now our family was burgeoned with seven new babies.

Needless to say, the birth of our seven kittens aroused great interest in our neighborhood and among our students. Everyone wanted to see our kittens. They slept comfortably in a huge, padded wicker basket in David's bedroom.

Many children wanted to have a kitten. So we had to set up some rules. If you wanted to have one of our kittens, you needed to present a letter of permission from your parents. After two months the kittens were ready to be placed with eager families. Reluctantly, we first allowed Figaro, a black and white charmer, to be with a family with several children.

Tommy Fitzgerald begged to have one of our kittens. One day his mother telephoned us, wondering if we felt Tommy really needed a kitten to make his life complete. The Fitzgeralds picked Winner, a beautiful angora. For sixteen years the family sent us Christmas cards with Winner's photo included. She was a long liver just like her mother, Pansy.

We found loving homes for all the kittens. Sport was the last to leave. All the kittens departed with a can of special cat food and a box of Meow Mix. One rainy night Sport's mother rang our front doorbell and told us she had to return Sport because she had to go on an extended trip to Europe. We were overjoyed to take Sport back and Pansy welcomed him, too.

We traveled to our summer home at Sebago Lake in Maine, taking the kittens with us. They traveled in their large wicker basket and caused quite a stir when placed in the back window of our car.

Nora, our cleaning lady, was quite happy when our kittens all found homes because we had so many visitors all wanting to see and play with the kittens. They were what she called "an attractive nuisance" to her.

Pansy was very playful when she was young. Whenever I was practicing putting indoors in our study, she would run after the golf ball before it could make it into the cup.

Perhaps one of Pansy's favorite activities was visiting one of our classrooms where students were working. When she got lonely, she would put her paw under the classroom door and jiggle the door until it opened. Then she would jump up on the table. First, she would sit at the head of the table and look around to survey what the students were doing. Then she would walk over and spread her body over the material (usually a book). Then Janemarie would say, "Pansy, you must let Billy do his work." She would look at me as if to say, "Who, me?" Of course, the students loved her act. Then I would have to take her under my arm, go downstairs, and give her a saucer of milk. The activity took place regularly for a number of years and always delighted the students.

Pansy was a great traveler to our Maine summer home. She loved to roam in the woods and bring back mice and an occasional chipmunk as a present to us. When we had to return to our home in Arlington, Massachusetts, she would disappear as if she had a sixth sense about our departure from the lake. At the end of one weekend, we could not find her, and she had to stay with our neighbors, the Coles. She enjoyed her extended vacation.

One day a large dog chased her up a very tall tree. After shooing the dog away, David had to climb up our extension ladder and rescue her from a precarious location on the top rung of the ladder, with one hand reaching for her and the other hand clinging to the ladder. Fortunately she trusted David to be her rescuer.

As Pansy grew older, she slowed up and became increasingly content to sit in our laps and remain inside. She still welcomed students to our reading clinic from her perch on top of the radiator cover at the entrance to our home. She still awaited the petting strokes from students. If one failed to stroke her, she let out a plaintive "Meow," refusing to be ignored.

Pansy lived for twenty-one years. Her departure left a tremendous void not only in our lives, but in our hearts. As a tribute to Pansy for sure it is no surprise to say that she will live far beyond her own demise.

THE RESTAURANT WITH THE SIDEWALK CAFÉ

Giuseppi Losurdo is a gutsy guy. He is also a survivor. Presently he is the owner of Anthony's Pizza at 890 Mass. Avenue, across from Stop and Shop in Arlington, Massachusetts.

He was born in Messina, Sicily, forty years ago. That city was destroyed in 1908 by an earthquake, tidal waves, and fires. Eventually it rose from its own ashes mostly with such imports as fruits, wine, oil, and silk.

While Arlington recently celebrated its 350th anniversary, Messina was observing its 1700th; not to talk of Rome, of course, that is 2700 years of age. In comparison, our history pales into yesterday.

When I questioned this entrepreneur about his boyhood, he recalls, "I loved Sicily, but I had to leave to make a better life. I left school when I was nine. I loved to play soccer. We, though, didn't have enough lira to buy a ball. So we pulled old, worn-out socks and pressed them together and made our own ball. That was good enough for us. We still had fun." His broken English causes him to miss a word now and then. No matter; he still speaks two languages.

269

Giuseppi was not richly endowed when he first came to America. "You know I had to pay Alitalia $550 to get here, and I had only 75 cents left to my blessed name. Not a very good way to begin a new life." That was his "Operation Shoestring" that didn't last too long.

He and his wife, Maria, start working at 7:00 a.m. from Monday to Saturday and close their restaurant every night at 9:00 p.m. That's a fourteen hour day, no matter how you look at it. Whew! They begin making their own home-made sauces and preparing their chicken, meat-balls, and veal. Everything comes served with its own generosity and thoughtfulness.

While Maria usually stays in the kitchen (she knows how to take the heat), Giuseppi takes care of the waiting customers. He is the one who makes things happen. I was over-whelmed by his sense of duty. He tells me, "The big thing in business is pride. Pride is what counts in life. Pride means working hard. It means pleasing your customers, too."

I watch Maria work in the kitchen. Her hands move in rapid gestures that tell me more than any words she could have spoken. She is always on the move making this and cooking that. The atmosphere in the restaurant is light and entertaining. Among voices I hear, "Hold the onions on the baconburger!"

You may have whatever you like at Anthony's

at breakfast, lunch, or dinnertime. Anyone for pasta or pizza for the palate? The coffee comes free each day at breakfast from 8:00 to 11:00 a.m. That's a good attention-getter. What would you like for breakfast? Pancakes? French toast?

Or maybe your stomach is ready for delicious eggs and sausages? Or eggs and ham? Perhaps you might prefer a cheese or western omelet along with toasted homefries? I settle for toast, a little bacon and however-I-would-like-my-eggs-to-be-or-not-to-be.

For lunch you may request any pizzas (just the way your mother thought she made them), or subs that come in all sorts of combinations. And when it's Italian, how about ziti, ravioli or spaghetti? In fact, if you need calzone, Giuseppi will get it for you. Would you be interested in a crispy fish platter? A hot fudge sundae? To go or not to go? At least, how about a banana split sundae to round off your lunch? Or is that your favorite dessert? How does that possess you?

I'm certain that if you ask for a cucumber and pimento salad, high on flavor, low on cost, or a full bodied shrimp and fettuccine et alia, he would instantly prepare it for you.

I dare say it's hard to know why life, when the plot accumulates, is so ineluctably tied up with the chosen ordeal of food. Everything comes full blast a la carte or a la mode. The heart may have its salivary reasons, but I honestly think that unreasonable reason unswervingly crouches like a fierce dog at its gate:

> You watch your weight
> And watch it grow
> Beyond its present
> Status quo,
> For eating's such
> A secret sin
> By letting all
> That food go in.

Maria remembers when she used to make her own clothes for her family. Dresses and curtains too. She is relieved to announce, "Now I don't have to stitch and sew like I used to do. Giuseppi and I don't have to work a 20 hour day anymore. Now it's much easier. We work only a 14 hour day. Never is there enough time in the day to do everything."

After the Fresh Touch Cleaners was destroyed by fire, Anthony's was lucky to be in business. Thanks must go to the Arlington Fire Department for their deliverance. The business was shut down for a day. Giuseppi told me it was a close shave. He did, however, have to get rid of about $500 worth of food that had spoiled from all the smoke. So he was happy with his sense of fate. The Losurdos live in Billerica and have three children. Anthony, 19, is a freshman at Middlesex Community College; he hopes to go into the business world. Tindoro is 17, a senior at Billerica High, and expects to attend an architectural school in Boston. Gioseppina is 15 and her ambition is to become a lawyer some day. Giuseppi showed me a snapshot of his beautiful home.

Anthony's is a family restaurant. When the children get out of school, they rush to rally around their mom and dad. By getting involved, they make the business run more smoothly. Giuseppi realizes how tough it is because he is aware of so many businesses that come and die too quickly.

Giuseppi supports the town's softball teams. He advertises in the *Arlington Advocate*, and he pays his monthly rent. Nevertheless, his business improves bit by bit each day. There is an elemental need in Giuseppi's spirit, "Anyone who believes in luck is out of luck. There is no such thing as luck in the business world. But I know there is such a thing as hard work. That's all I ever need to know."

I ask Giuseppi another question, "Do you get much business from high school students?" He tells me about some students who were in his restaurant one day. He was curious, "What are you kids up to? What, no school? Aren't you supposed to be in school?" He tells me they made up some silly excuses. The students don't bother him anymore since the school has gotten stricter about kids cutting classes. He welcomes students to his restaurant. He just doesn't like to have kids around if they are supposed to be in school; that's the strict father in Giuseppi.

Giuseppi's ideas go beyond emotions and the narrow niches. There is no hair-splitting argument here. He follows his formula: it is called "minding the store."

Last year he appealed to the board of selectmen to receive approval for an outdoor café. He reflects, "It was a tense moment, but I had to fight for what I believed in. Now I am proud of the fact that I have the only sidewalk café in the town of Arlington."

When he won his appeal, he was as jubilant as a boxer who had just received his greatest artistic triumph. You have to rise very early in the morning if you think that you can ever hope to beat Giuseppi to the punch.

Anthony's Pizza may not be apple pie, but it is America and America is spaghetti, pizza, gnocchi, pasta and whatever else besides. Giuseppi asks his familiar question, "What would you like today, handsome?" His agreeable personality and his black, roly poly eyes provide a lot of magic for Anthony's success.

Finally, I ask them both, "When do you get away for a vacation?" They tell me that their vacation is with their children. If there is time, they will go with them anywhere they suggest. Giuseppi thinks for a while and then speaks out, "Oh, yes, my vacation is also getting my garden ready for spring— my carrots, tomatoes, squash and beans."

If energy and motivation have anything to do with success, then their business has already made it. The Losurdos will tell you there is no easy way to make a fortune. Instead, they will tell you there is a hard and honest way to make a living.

Anthony's star is rising up and outward. Business is getting better. So is life. Grazie, Maria, Giuseppi, and family!

A STORY FOR THE SPORTS-MINDED: 1956

First of all, I shall give you an insight into the Marathon by telling you its short but dignified history. The story of the Race from Marathon is one of the most stirring the world has ever heard. It originates in Greece in 490 B.C. It brings us back to one of the first decisive battles in the world's history between the Persians on one side and the Athenians on the other. The Persian armies are advancing upon the helpless little city of Athens. The rulers of Athens need help; they send for Pheidippides, their champion runner, who has won his myrtle crown at the famous Olympic Games which were held by the Greek states. Incidentally, the victor of the Boston Marathon always receives a myrtle crown which, until a few years ago, used to come directly from Greece for this occasion. They command Pheidippides to run and ask help from the Spartans. He runs for two days and two nights, swimming rivers and climbing the mountains in his path. Pheidippides then runs back once more to Athens. The Persians have now landed and the Athenians come out in force to fight them. The tired and worn-out Pheidippides takes his long spear and shield and marches with the 10,000 picked men to meet the enemy. The importance of this Battle of Marathon is how the 10,000 Greeks drove back hundreds of thousands of Persians, but the greater significance is the story of Pheidippides. The victorious Greeks call upon him to bring back the news of the victory to Athens. Throwing aside his shield and spear, he runs over hills and dales from Marathon to Athens, a distance of 26 miles. He reaches the Gates of Athens and falling into the arms of friends, shouts out: "Rejoice, we conquer," and so the gallant runner dies.

The marathon, over 2,000 years old, is considered to be perhaps the only true amateur contest remaining in this growing age of commercialized sport. In the U.S. the BAA Marathon in Boston is the biggest spectacle in the sports calendar, when 1 million people gather along a 26.2 mile route between Hopkinton to Exeter Street to goggle at 200 human oddities who squirm, waddle, lope and twitch . . . and all of this for what? It is for the chance—someone's chance to be crowned with a sprig of laurel. The rest are rewarded with the traditional orders of beef stew, but outside of that, they get nothing out of it, virtually nothing. This has been going on each April 19th for 59 years, bringing men from all parts of the world, from Japan, Sweden, England, Korea, France, and Italy, to name some foreign countries. People are often curious why marathoners gallop 26.2 miles over highway roads with only a ghost of a chance of winning. They come from all walks of life, from the everyday worker to even fields of medicine, law, education, business and ministry. These marathoners have a lot in common; they are a happy breed. They come to win or lose a race in a sportsmanlike manner; they remain the same, regardless of race, color or creed. They are friendly toward each other and are willing to make sacrifices for each other. These men are classified in three ways: first—the few who win and are rewarded, second—those who run a few miles and then become passengers in cars for the rest of the journey, and third—the great number who continue to run with stomach cramps, headaches, heel blisters, and sensations of hot-lead up their spines.

The question remains unanswered. Why do they run? Is it to escape temporary obscurity? Maybe to dream of attaining celebrity status? The majority of runners have no possible chance to dominate the field. They plod along listening to their hearts beat, sweating, fuming, swallowing water and finally staggering home hours after the race is over. Clarence Demar,

68 years old, who, after 45 years of plodding the BAA marathon, expresses it well. He says that no drudge is too great to smother a marathoner's single purpose. Some people like to fish, some like to watch a game of football, others like to drive a baseball over the fence. But marathoners like to see their feet move. Their real reason for running is simply for the joy, for the love of it; for them it is a sense of achievement and satisfaction in completing the marathon.

I shall now spend some time on details about the marathon in order to clear up a few of its misconceptions. One of the most discussed topics in sport is the question: Is running hard on the heart? This is something which the average person, athlete, parent, and many doctors, trainers and coaches know very little about. But every definite proof has been compiled by physical education and medical authorities that running, no matter how strenuous, will not injure or harm a healthy, normal heart. In most cases it will slightly increase the size of the heart, but this is supposed to have beneficial rather than detrimental effects. But, of course, no person with an organic murmur or any other organic injury or disease should take part in running, or do any very hard physical work. Actually running is a heart conditioner and strengthener.

There is an old wives' tale about the terrible dangers of developing athlete's heart. The athletes are supposed to die a few years after retirement. The idea that several years of tough running competition will make a person more liable to a heart attack or heart disease has been proved to be absolutely false, for marathons are a test of the heart and circulation whereas sprints are a test of muscles. The successful marathoner trains in the methods which develop his heart and his muscles. The human body can take any amount of strenuous exercise and, unless it is taxed to the limit, it will not improve. Herein is found the real science of training—to bring oneself to the point of exhaustion periodically and not waste time training past that point is learned through experience. Muscles including the heart grow and remain strong while in use and rapidly go backward and grow weaker when not in use. I have found a comfortable training schedule; it consists of running and covering at least 60 miles weekly. With such exercise I, too, have developed an athlete's heart and don't feel unfortunate in doing so. For an athlete's heart is a stronger, more efficient organ which pumps more blood with fewer beats.

What usually happens to the body in a marathon? Do the athletes who take part in a sport of such extreme exertion injure their bodies? Is such a sport dangerous? The Canadian Marathon Championship on August 20th in Three Rivers, Quebec is a very good example. In running this race heat was generated, and like an engine, the body works best when it is hot, for then the muscles are looser, and the action of running is supposedly freer. But sometimes the conditions are unfavorable to the heat that is being lost, as in a marathon on a very hot and humid day, and then the temperature of the body may rise beyond all physical limits, and the heat-regulating part of the body may be strained, resulting perhaps in sun-stroke and finally in collapse. Collapse in long-distance events may be caused by the exhaustion of the sugar reserves in the body, but I doubt it if the body is injured or strained with permanent consequences. The eyes become tired, and collapse may temporarily affect their condition. For example, when Bannister became the first to break the 4 minute mile, he collapsed at the finish and for awhile was even color-blind. This is a true statement and goes to explain why the condition of your eyes may indeed affect your general health.

As a result of physical training, the muscles of the heart become stronger and are able to pump more blood at each beat. The heart rate returns to its normal level much more quickly in the person who trains than in the one who doesn't. In marathon races it is more common practice for contestants to consume salt and some sugar containing food at regular intervals. Sugar is the main fuel used during strenuous exercise and is capable of providing energy very quickly. With long-distance running, the amount of sugar in the body is scarce, and the body weakens and harmful effects may occur. But if sugar is supplied, this condition may be corrected. The body must also be supplied with an adequate amount of salt in order that it can work properly rather than be exhausted. Water, too, is essential; water is lost through perspiration, and it is important that the water content of the body be maintained at a constant level, since loss of water may produce great damage. The correct rule to follow is to take a drink whenever one is thirsty but never to take a lot of water at any one time during a race.

I've been asked a number of questions by some curious people. They ask me if and when I get my "second wind." The medical profession is not real certain just what second wind is, but they know that such a thing exists. What happens, for instance, is that when running along the road, I may feel terrible, experiencing the unpleasant "can't breathe" sensation, plus a headache and a tight chest. Then if I keep going, this feeling gradually disappears. I begin to feel better, and my breathing becomes more regulated. This is known as second wind.

Athletes sometimes get stitches when they are running. These stitches are sensations located in the lower rib region where the liver is situated. A stitch may cause tenderness in the muscles and may, in turn, bring on a muscular cramp. Stitches probably result from lack of proper diet and a feeling of being out of condition, but the better the conditioning, the fewer the stitches.

There are wonderful opportunities ahead for the youth of Newfoundland if they take advantage of them. If they are willing to work hard and keep their interests high, there are many fields to conquer and many records to break. We can do this if we put our utmost into proper training and the organization of more competition. The idea is always to keep trying to break records and never become satisfied with our efforts. By using this system, I have improved and will continue to do so because I am greatly interested and have an inspiration that will spur me on to greater heights. It shows just what can be done if we are willing to work hard and train faithfully. The man who works the hardest is the man who usually wins, for hard work is the secret of success. One important thing I have learned through my running experience is that a person can achieve any goal, if he is willing to work hard enough for it.

Nothing is unattainable, it's strictly up to you, for all things are possible to the one who works hard and has faith in himself.

If a person wants to become a champion, he should realize that he must be determined and have the courage to train, practice and work as hard as he can, until he reaches his peak of condition. For he will only achieve his goal in athletics by grueling, sweating exertion. There is no greater thrill than to compete when in perfect condition. In fact, in most events, condition is 75% of the battle, and the man with the best condition is usually the winner.

I am keeping my eyes on the future and with repeated practice and hard training over long periods of time, I hope to win some Canadian and American Championships and, above all, to fulfill my greatest sports ambition by representing Canada in the 1956 Olympics.

Homer, the famous Greek poet, once wrote in his poem, *The Odyssey*, that there is no greater glory for a man as long as he lives than that which he wins by his own hands and feet. Man's glory of achievement "by his own hands and feet," which the Greeks praised so highly in their Games, continues to grow. Steadily, by split seconds and fractions of inches, athletes push themselves toward greater and greater performances, so much so that we almost believe that there is no limit in athletics.

ONCE UPON A TIME WHEN RUNNERS WERE YOUNG

It was only for a moment. We ran in the world
for bolder comprehension. What the mind
wanted, the heart, too, craved. Running was
endless reaching out to attain something that
lay beyond.

Perhaps it was finding oneself sufficiently
strong and able. We looked at the sun touching
upon the horizon as it brought its light over the
top of Signal Hill. How we made the earth
shake and tremble with our feet!

Desire was more and more or not at all.
It had to come to raise us all to beat out time.
But every second of it was enough to terrify us.
Hope at least was irresistible and hallowing
when the body at times cried out in making
its sacrifice for being.

The Lord in His mercy told us that the race
was forever to claim the sublime integrity
of saints.
Our feet lit now here and then there, always
lifting up and on and on and far beyond while

the heart sought perfection for the sake
of individuality.

Identity was the thing. The pride was in
competing. That was the nature of the ego
for glory man-made-manifest.
Our eyes were molded in fire and our feet
were bright as gold.
Even our souls were captivated for awhile.
Beauty was the mode and love was as vast
as the universe.
Remember: our bodies were in the bloom
of flesh.

Memory mirrors back the pulse that fashioned
our goals.
Yes! It was true. The earth touched our very
being.
We penetrated it till the heart stretched out to
the breaking point.
No stopping for breath though the conscience
recognized the inherent danger.

It was hard when the body was like a candle
spent.
Fatigue was the dead and awful silence:
the murderous conspiracy framing us against
its horror.
The problem was that time moved without
making the faintest noise.

Covertly we glanced at our opponents who
had hungry, superstitious eyes.
Nothing there to our taste or liking
Waiting for the gun to go off was eternity.
We knew or dared to know that we'd win
for victory was the harvest waiting to be won.

BOSTON MARATHON

To Boston from the heights of Hopkinton,
Those gallant energetic souls,
With such strong instincts to run on and on,
Fulfill in splendor their distinctive goals.

Racing hearts beat like drums as time ticks by,
To pay homage to god, Pheidippides;
Parched parted lips evoke a frenzied sigh,
When worn-out muscles support weary knees.

Thoughts of rigor mortis provide no thrill
As some lose their rhythm, others feel pain,
Responding to torture on Heartbreak Hill,
That measures survival by how they train.

Glory to the winner, praise to the rest,
For victory's judged in one's state of mind;
Champions are those who endure the test,
Content to keep running though far behind.

EXPERIENCING THE BRITISH EMPIRE GAMES

It was indeed a great pleasure to represent Canada in the 1954 British Empire Games at Vancouver. After six years of competitive running, I have reached one of my most important goals. The Canadian marathon Trials at Hamilton, Ontario on June 19 provided the decision. I trained hard for this race. I covered well over 800 miles, but, most of my workouts were done in cool weather, in low temperatures ranging from 50 to 60 degrees. In Hamilton, on the day of the race, it was very much warmer; the temperature was up to 90 degrees. I found myself doing well up to the 20 mile mark where I was more than a mile ahead of the field and then shortly after, I was stricken by the heat and collapsed from its power. But, later, in view of my withdrawal from the race, I found that my efforts were not in vain but were, in time, rewarded.

Lord Alexander, one of the most popular Governor-Generals ever to represent the Crown in Canada arrived in Vancouver and presided at the colorful opening ceremonies at the gigantic track and field stadium. Alexander read the traditional opening message from the British Empire and Commonwealth's chief patron, the Queen. Then the parade of athletes took place in all its pageantry. Each contingent was dressed in its official uniform; preceded by a shield bearing the name of its country. It is then accompanied by its national flag. The National anthem is then sung, the parade leaves the Stadium and the Games officially open. This, the biggest and most impressive Empire and Commonwealth show of all is over now, but I'll never forget it. In truth, I shall always cherish its fond memories.

What was the purpose of this great sporting occasion? Its significance lay in the fact that the ties of the Empire were strengthened, and it also provided the tradition that amateurism still lives on in this growing age of sport. It was, assuredly, a most friendly, family occasion.

The first day of the Games showed the fine successes of England, particularly in track, and Australia dominating the swimming. The major triumphs of Canada, the host country, came in the rowing and in Doug Hepburn's weightlifting. It showed Mike Agostini of Trinidad winning the 100 yards in 9.6 seconds. He possessed an amazing stride for being only 5½ feet tall. The three mile race, the greatest race of its kind ever run, was won by Chris Chataway in the splendid time of

13 minutes 35 seconds. In that same race was an athlete from Kenya, Maiyoro, who ran bare-footed all the way and came in 4th in very good time. The high jump was one of the most thrilling events in its day with Africa winning 1st, 2nd and 3rd places. A Nigerian medical student, lfeatjuna, by name, just over 5 feet tall, tried to jump 6 feet 8 inches. He made a cat-like approach, ran and sprang upwards and cleared the bar and succeeded thus in jumping 14 inches above his own height, something never before achieved in athletic history.

The final day before a packed audience of 35,000 in the magnificent new Empire Stadium, was one that has never been surpassed in the history of athletics. The miracle mile in which world-record holder John Landy led all the way except for the last 200 yards when he felt Roger Bannister closing in. As the two milers were nearing the tape, thousands cheered, and the excitement rose feverishly. Landy looked over his inside shoulder, but at that same moment Bannister was running past on the outside and putting on what is known as his "finishing kick." He finished in 3 minutes 5.8 seconds and Landy in 3 minutes 59.5 seconds. The mood of exhilaration brought about by this miracle mile race was however short-lived. For a few minutes later it was followed by the tragedy of marathoner, Jim Peters, who collapsed 10 or 11 times on reaching the Stadium, and made a valiant but vain and pitiful effort to reach the finish line which was only 220 yards away.

The drama of the world's greatest milers again breaking the 4 minute barrier and of Peters' staggering into the stadium in an unconscious condition brought the 5th British Empire Games to a dramatic close. Canada has never seen anything like it before. In nine days records were smashed everywhere, and the final day, with the mile and marathon, eclipsed everything. It was such a stirring spectacle that triple winners and record-breaking became unimportant. The Duke of Edinburgh was in the royal stand on the last day when the team captains passed in final review and lowered their nations' flags in the elaborate and extremely moving closing ceremonies. The Duke summed up the Games and said, "I hope every one of you who lived at the athletes' village will be able to go home and say you know we are a family of nations." The last day was filled with such glory and pageantry that the memory of it will be a sacred treasure for Canada and all other nations.

Lastly, the British Empire Games personified Baron de Coubertin's credo: "The important thing in life is not the triumph but the struggle.

The essential thing is not to have conquered but to have fought well." I was pleased to have placed 5th in the marathon and received two points for Canada.

A DREAM DEFERRED

October 18, 1956
Mr. K.K. Yost
593 Spruce Street
Winnipeg, Manitoba

Dear Mr. Yost:

I remember your visit to St. John's, Newfoundland, two years ago and how much I enjoyed meeting you. I am no longer in St. John's since I am presently at Boston University with a leadership scholarship. I am writing to you with the sincere hope that you will be able to explain why I have not been notified about anything pertaining to the official selection of the members of Canada's Olympic Team.

I was so pleased to have defended my Canadian Marathon Championship successfully and to have won the official Canadian Marathon Olympic Trial. I am disappointed, though, in not having reached the standard time—just 65 seconds short of it. My time in winning the marathon was 2 hours 36 minutes 5 seconds which broke the Hamilton course record.

I was reminded by Hamilton track officials that my time would have been equivalent to 2 hours and 25 minutes on the Boston Marathon course. I understand the Hamilton course is considered "slow" compared to other courses. Also the weather was hot and certainly not conducive to the best running conditions. I was also informed that my time was one of the fastest ever recorded on this Hamilton course. The long grind on a hot day took its heavy toll as only nine of the eighteen starters could finish this race.

The favorite in this marathon was a Hamiltonian, Gordon Dickson, who dropped out from heat exhaustion. Then I took the lead and won the race with the second place finisher about 14 minutes behind me. The Hamilton newspapers stated that there was a likely possibility that I would be named to the Canadian Olympic Team that travels to Melbourne, Australia, in November. Mr. Neil Farrell informed me that after the race, Mr. Harold Colby had forwarded the results to Mr. F.N. Rowell with the recommendation that I be picked for the team.

Evidently, nothing further was heard from Mr. Rowell until an article appeared in the newspapers that Miss Whitty and other members had been selected instead of me. Mr. Farrell found it unusual that Miss Whitty would be selected, since she never made the qualifying standard in her high jumping trial.

Mr. Farrell also mentioned that he, as an official, and others, were supposed to vote to see who will represent Canada in the marathon. I had proven myself to have won even under the most trying conditions. Now I also find that three other athletes were picked, according to the newspapers; those three who never made their official standards either. They were, namely: Doug Clement, Laird Sloan, and Dorothy Kozak.

Four committee members were supposed to vote in this decision, and four of them would have voted for me, but all four of them were excluded from the voting process. Mr. Rowell was a one-man committee member who made the fateful decision by himself.

I was greatly disturbed over those proceedings, when I consider all the time and effort I had put forth in training for this Olympic Trial. The officials should have taken into consideration that the race was run in the heat. I am certain if the weather had been a little cooler, I would have made much better time.

Since May I had ample time and opportunity to train conscientiously. In six months I had logged over 1400 miles before the Olympic Marathon Trial. I sincerely hope that all my time and effort are not in vain, for it has been my great sporting ambition to become Canada's representative for the marathon in the Melbourne Olympics.

I have been told it would be best to have my branch of the AAU in St. John's, Newfoundland make an appeal on my behalf by offering the necessary expenses for the trip, if that were possible. I would like to get your opinion on this matter. Currently, I am running in cross country dual meets at B.U. and am still training conscientiously with the hope that I will be named to that Canadian team.

I would sincerely appreciate if the contents of this letter were made known to Mr. Ken Farmer, President of the Canadian Olympic Association, in his official capacity. Also, I would like to hear from you about my possibility for selection. So far I have not heard from any official source as to what's going on in this critical matter. Thank you for your kind attention to this letter.

Yours truly,

George Hillier
Arlington, Massachusetts

Unfortunately, there was no response to my letter. The Newfoundland Branch of the Amateur Athletic Union of Canada sent a formal protest to the Canadian Olympic Association over the manner in which I was eliminated from the Olympic team.

I told the Newfoundland AAU Branch that I missed the qualifying time for the marathon. Also, I had the votes from the Selection Committee to represent Canada, but the Committee Chairman, Fred Rowell, decided against me and chose high jumper, Alice Whitty, who never made the qualifying height in her event.

It would have been more helpful if the Canadian Olympic Association had taken the heat of the day into consideration when the marathon was run. Of course, I was devastated by my being rejected, yet I finally adjusted to my fate and continued with my life, looking more optimistically to the future. For sure, I appreciated Mr. Joey Smallwood, Newfoundland's Premier, who said: "This matter is intolerable and, if I had my way, I would charter a plane myself for George Hillier so he could fulfill his Olympic dream in Melbourne, Australia."

A RUNNER REWARDED

I hope I'm not being overly pretentious, but on Thursday, July 16, 2009, I was inducted into the Newfoundland and Labrador Hall of Fame for my running achievements in the 1950's.

Indeed, I was quite pleased with what the selection committee said about yours truly: "George Hillier was one of the finest middle and long-distance runners Newfoundland and Labrador has ever produced. During his career, Hillier, who was born in St. John's, Newfoundland, held records in the one mile, three mile, six mile, fifteen mile, and the 26.2 mile marathon."

"He competed successfully in cross-country running, tennis, table tennis, and was no stranger to walking races. In all his athletic endeavors, he earned a reputation for always displaying exceptional sportsmanship and showing the very highest regard for all others involved in any event in which he was associated. He was simply a fine athlete and a true gentleman."

"His long distance running career started in the late 1940's and his first victory came in *The Evening Telegram* 10-mile event. He won the *Telegram* ten miler for seven successive years and placed first in *The Daily News* Marathon in '51, '53, '54, and '55. He placed first in the one mile in 1951 and 1953 and was winner of the half-mile competition in 1951."

"He excelled nationally, again by demonstrating the skill and talent that he displayed at the provincial and local levels."

"Hillier was first among the Canadian entries in the 1955 Canadian Marathon at Trois Rivieres, Quebec, and in 1956 won the Canadian Marathon Championship in Hamilton, Ontario. In the 1954 British Empire Marathon Trials, heat exhaustion forced him out of the competition after he held first place for 20 miles. This performance gained him a place on Canada's national marathon team and at an international race, he finished fifth. He moved to Boston, Massachusetts, in 1955, and continued his marathon running. He was 19th in the 1955 Boston Marathon and placed 25th against an internationally renowned field in 1956."

"He was twice voted St. John's Athlete of the Year for 1954 and 1955."

I thought it most proper to thank the selection committee for their many contributions:

As a Newfoundland runner in the 1950's, I would like to publicly thank Bob Walsh, NLAA President, for his encouraging words for the newly inducted members of the Newfoundland and Labrador Hall of Fame.

Also, my deep gratitude to Dee Murphy, Wulf Stender, and David Carroll for serving on the Hall of Fame's Selection Committee. Indeed, it was a distinct honor to have Geoff Babstock as my presenter who paid such a kind tribute to my athletic achievements.

As a loyal Newfoundlander, I feel at this time I must recognize and appreciate the numerous friends and supporters who have helped me through the years. Without them, I could not have had such a successful career.

Although I now live in another country, my Newfoundland roots run deep. No matter where I live, I find Newfoundlanders love the spirit of competition that sports provide. In the early years, we were the veritable pioneers in running. We ran the Tely Ten in small numbers to win or, at least, to improve on our times. Yet today the numbers have grown remarkably into thousands.

I guess it doesn't matter in the long run who wins the race for they are all winners in my eyes:

> We ran to compete,
> We ran to run.
> We never ran for money,
> We ran for fun.

I like to remind you what the author, John Crosbie, said in his novel, *No Holds Barred*, "How do you recognize Newfoundlanders when you get to Heaven? They are the ones who always want to go home."

In closing, I must say I will always remain a true Newfoundlander in my heart and soul. Thank you and may God bless you all.

FROM THE DEPTHS OF A NIGHTMARE COME HOPE AND LIGHT

In August, 1995, I experienced the greatest shock of my life by coming down with cancer of the colon at the age of 65. Years ago, when I heard about anyone with cancer, I usually thought about death, someone dying or, at least, the shadow of some dark happening.

There are four stages of colon cancer; I was, unfortunately, in the third stage, commonly called Duke's C colon cancer. At this advanced stage, the cancer cells have already metastasized to nearby lymph nodes. I guess no one's luck lasts forever.

In the beginning, I felt oppressed by a villous-like tumor that moved inside my body; it was preparing to devour me. Then on August 9, fifteen centimeters of my sigmoid colon, along with the tumor, were removed from my large intestine. So, you see, cancer is my enemy. I hope to shake it off, but I have trouble because it follows me relentlessly like the shadow of some ancient sin.

I thought destiny was overpowering me. I saw a dark path I was to tread. I shrank back, doubtful of some infinite power to carry me through. I even felt suspended in the depths of impenetrable darkness. Fate had shut the door on me with a crash. I was alone with grief in an alien world.

In the darkness of the night, I thought about my future and wondered how much of it was left to me. Indeed, I was consoled by loneliness, the strange moods and the constant play of emotions. Anyway, it appeared to me that the control of my life had already passed out of my hands. My brain was numb. I was at the mercy of my fears and imaginings.

Every now and then the whole scene grew dim as though it were a fantasy and about to disappear. I realize I am beholden to my wife, Janemarie, two sons, four sisters, all their families, and all my friends and relatives. Gradually, I got steadier and emerged with motivation that one associates with reflection born of experience. My friends came through for me. They got me to look on the brighter side of life. They gave fresh meaning to my ways. They never failed to provide hope wherein love and the simplicity of prayer were at the heart of the matter.

Undoubtedly, my friends knew I was the vulnerable one. So they spoke to me and came to satisfy my deep desires by helping me find some measure of peace and contentment. I saw them with their good thoughts, their guidance and their dialogue beautiful in itself. I remember my friends as one remembers a pleasant dream dissolving the blurs of sharper memories that intervene. It was time for me to challenge cancer and the fear of death.

I am grateful to have recovered my senses. The broken phrases, questions, sighs, tears, and exclamations have all passed away. Suddenly, the words of an old hymn now echo in my mind: "There's a wideness to God's mercy, like the wideness of the sea."

From now on I will sanctify each moment as it comes. I am no longer in lamentation. When ecstasy arrives, nothing can dim the glitter of the stars. Now my chemotherapy that will last a year is no longer a drag. Instead, it has gotten to be a celebration. I look forward to my chemo with the combined drugs fluorouracil and levamisole recommended by my oncologist. My wife had done everything humanly possible to turn my life from a nightmare toward a dream. The dream goes on and on and every moment of every day becomes precious. I never fail to recite my daily prayers in my gratitude for being alive. With great gallantry, I praise God for bringing me back to reality after so many trials and errors. I recall the sacred song "Miserere" along with its distinct chant, "Have mercy, O Lord."

Ten-million Americans who were beset by cancer are walking today on the streets of America cancer-free. I am set to bear the weight of life's commitments. Though life is not always smooth sailing, I begin to salve my wounds. What is left for me, therefore, is not space, not seasons, not the presence of anything, not the coming and the going, but only the absence of suffering and that is truly love itself.

In the cool Florida nights, when the air chills the early mist, what is left is a heart that is never closed to hope. What's more, the sun always comes out in Florida. My life is strong enough to accept all the problems I have learned to endure. I turn to hope, and hope occupies my mind like a grain of sand in an oyster shell to be turned in the course of time into a pearl.

At this time in my life, I fall back on poetry for relief and pleasure, and I wish to know more about the how and why of the world. Though I am plagued with cancer, I have an inner need to live more deeply and to find out how I may help others who have to cope with their diseases. I am at home with the joy of a poem as I read *The Lake Isle of Innisfree*. This poem, by William Butler Yeats, is my favorite. I memorized all of it as a young boy in Saint John's, Newfoundland, many years ago. Yeats shows his sensitivity to the beauty of the outdoors and his awareness of the Irish fold. His words, drawn from the face of nature, always overwhelm me.

I have a message of hope for those who have cancer or any kind of disease. Hope is a poem about the vision of the Earth, thoughts of a journey, the memory of a city and the house where I was born, and the character who has the courage to fight my cancer. Words come to me like pickets on a fence: the fear of death and its uncomprehending mystery, a God waiting to take my breath away, a good-natured laugh, love and timeless skies, and a poem written by someone who makes the Earth cry out in its dwelling places of love.

I read Rilke, the elegant poet, who wills me not purity itself, but love and adventure. It's funny in a way when people ask me for the time; I am compelled to reply, "It's now or never!" I have a quiet time to listen to Enya, the Irish colleen, who sings her shepherd moons with a soft, affirmative voice that creates its own fusion and gives no quarter. I am entranced by her exquisite tone and faultless rhythm as she sings a song that turns the strange into the accessible:

"My life goes on in endless song
"Along Earth's lamentations,
"I hear the real, though far-off hymn

"That hails a new creation.
"Through all the tumult and the strife,
"I hear its music ringing,
"It sounds an echo in my soul.
"How can I keep from singing?"

I am preoccupied with getting better, and I do believe I will defeat this cancer in time. In the long run, nothing is lost except the crucible of sorrow and pain. After the long, interminable strain is over, I live with hope. I am alive, and I am content with the sense of freedom that gives me the greatest desire to love and smile at everyone.

Today is the day. I pray and speak to God in my own way so He will learn about the secret longings of the heart. I meditate and read from today's epistle. I take the inspired words into my mind and think profoundly on what they mean. Once I find a direction that is constant and unchanging, that is, when my questions are all answered, I shall always remember the voice. When I recognize that certain smile, I shall always remember the face. Perhaps the final happiness may lie beyond space where time will last forever.

EVEN FOR A FATALIST, LIFE GOES ON

You undergo your operation for colon cancer on August 10, 1995, at the Mercy Hospital in Portland, Maine. In so many words your surgeon, Dr. Radke, states that a segment of your colon, measuring fifteen centimeters in length, was removed during surgery and was found to reveal a villous-like tumor with finger-like projections.

In the autumn of the year you miss nothing of the passing scene. You are especially grateful for the many get-well cards, letters, telephone calls, balloons, flowers, and a book on miracle-cancer cures.

You thank your wife, Janemarie, for keeping up your spirits. You cannot live without her. After five days in hospital you return home to Sebago Lake in Naples, Maine, to recuperate.

In time you walk in the pine woods of the park where shifting sunlight dapples mossy trunks. The beech trees are sleekly gray as moose fur. In the quiet of the day you often come here alone to think.

You have a thought. You lose it. You find it again like a fragment of an old tune to remember: "Accentuate the positive, eliminate the negative, and latch on to the affirmative— don't mess with Mr. In-Between."

You scarcely believe in the reality of the scene before you: the pagan glare of a crackling fire and the old-timer, a bent figure of a man, who watches the brush burn brightly in the park. He heaps more sticks on the fire as if he were following some mysterious rite. The fire makes its hissing complements to the wind. As you walk on the beach you find chips of flint are left where arrowheads once upon a time were sharpened.

Two weeks later time suddenly turns defiant because your surgeon, who usually smiles when he sees you, is not smiling now. He says you have cancer of the colon according to the macroscopic examination; it's like saying the surgery was a success, but the patient almost died. When you first hear the news, your spirit shrinks like leaves that frost can shrivel in a single night.

So you believe nothing is certain though you always ate the cancer-fighting vegetables; you, the veritable one who thought you were safe; you, the high-fiber, low-fat man.

Nothing is guaranteed. Nothing is permanent. Nothing except dying, of course, and this is the thing you must learn how to fight. This is your challenge if time means anything to you. Each ache must find its own means for healing. You will need all the courage you have in order to survive.

What is the sentence brought before you? Dr. Radke recommends chemotherapy for one year with the drugs: five-fluorouracil and levamisole. Hopefully, these drugs will decrease the chance of tumor recurrence and survival with cancer that has already metastasized to nearby lymph nodes.

For a while you thought you were looking at life through iron bars. After the initial shock, you settle down.

You believe, anyway, optimists live longer than pessimists. It's amazing, in retrospect, how adaptable you become after having heard the horrid news from your doctor.

When Janemarie and you leave his office, you speak to her with consummate skill, "Now that we got those things squared away, where do we go for lunch?" Tolerance is such an asset when you do what you can to keep your flag flying.

From what you know you begin to think more about quality of time rather than quantity of years. You are a fatalist. Life goes on.

There's nothing better than the autumn of the year: the exuberance of colors, the red, orange, yellow, the fading green, and the gray. All the colors are there, even splotches of blue and indigo and traces of violet, if you search hard enough. The poet tells you this scene is the soul of it all, the beauty of nature and your love for life.

As you sit upon your chair on the beach, you wonder. You can't help it, but you wonder at the wonder of it all. The sun comes out brilliantly and the sky turns blue. Your world is mystical and calm. All the colors around you come together like a kaleidoscopic portrait of Mother Nature.

Is there, do you think, a poet, old and wise, who will pray for your deliverance or a God for old times' sake? The pastoral scene bursts upon your consciousness. Most of the leaves have already fallen and lie still around your feet. You no longer call it the Fall anymore. You call it the Autumn of the year. Sounds less agonizing, doesn't it?

Your oncologist, Dr. Hayes, tells you that your curability is at 50 percent, whereas, one year's chemo may add 20 percent more to your lifeline. So you go for it. As a teacher, you realize 70 percent, a C-, is passing; at least it's much better than a D or F.

In your visualization you become Robert the Bruce, King of Scotland, from the fact and legend as definite as the spider clears the intricate maze of its own making. You must remind yourself that cancer of the body is not cancer of the soul.

You remember your brother, John, fighting for his life and dying of cancer. You will never forget his brave farewell. Then, too, you dwell on your uncle, Jack Hillier, one of the Newfoundland soldiers who helped to save Monchy-Le-Preux from the Germans in the First World War. He was shot out of a bunker and lived to tell the tale.

The soldier comes out in you as you take up the sword. You find your uniform that hangs like a gray ghost somewhere in the corner of your mind. You still wear yesterday's scars and souvenirs of your fighting days.

You're sitting on a chair in your chemo room and being obliged as you watch the chemo nurses with their constant smiling faces, ready to shoot you up. You are tied to a bag for a year; a bag of sweet poison drip, drip, dripping into your foreign body so you can beat out those cancer cells.

You observe the faces of those you meet and you feel sorry for the sallow-looking ones with their sad expressions.

In your journey you will never forget those who fought hard down to the wire till death fulfilled its metaphor. As you look with a touch of pathos in your eyes, you will remember them at the epiphany's closing.

This is your last day at the Maine Center for Cancer Medicine. This is graduation day and you hope to receive your diploma, but you're not really certain what will happen. Who knows with cancer?

You're sitting on a chair and your oncologist, Dr. Tracey Weisberg, smiles at you, "I'm pleased to tell you—you're cancer-free!"

You are beside yourself with tears of joy. You rise from your chair and hug the doctor and kiss her on the cheek, of course, with a subtle sense of grace. She understands. Such happiness brings tears to your eyes, since love only knows why a grown man cries.

And now it's springtime and there is life and there is love with its redeeming smile.

TO JANEMARIE

When I was sick
you were so kind;
in such despair
you changed my mind.
You came to me
when I shed tears
and made me strong
to fight those fears.
I'm thankful friend
you knew my plight
and came in time
to help that night.

REFLECTIONS: OVERCOMING CANCER

The God who loves you, loves you more
than you will ever know. The surgeon's knife
brings on healing. A year of chemotherapy
ends.
Your dealing with fear is right on target.
Fear knocked on your door. Faith answered.
No one was there. Now you listen to your
oncologist, every word she says. She speaks
resolutely:
"You are cancer free!" You rise in gratitude
to thank her. A force thrusts itself upon you,
and what you think about beyond imagining,
begins. Sheer ecstasy takes over. Hope
arrives in the depth of time. Life comes
around full circle. Your face brightens as
if some light plays over it. You are deeply
moved and lost in meditation. Your eyes
fill with tears, but tears of joy. You get to
learn enough about the night and its secret
rhythm. You think of all you've fought for,
fought against, and won. You bless your
wife, two sons, four sisters, their families,
and all your friends and relatives. Then you
begin to realize the God you believe in is

the only hope you've got. You reach within yourself and find a song of praise, a hymn to birth, and love like a new world opens up before you.

ENRICHED BY INTENSIVE CARE

When I hold mortgage on my borrowed
    years
And have to pay whenever payment's due
For shocks with all their subtle trials and
    fears
Impel me toward those deeds I must pursue.
When in the cast of Florence Nightingale
Those nurses brought such healing with their
    light
And rose above the whimper and the wail
Throughout the chaos of the restless night.
So tangled up in such a web of strife
Yet love can conjure up more living breath
While duty bound to combat for my life
I save my soul for living and not death.
Is life then more than Heaven's Paradise
When glorious dreams endure before time
    dies?

MY TWO HEART ATTACKS

At the Mayo Clinic in Rochester, Minnesota, on January 21, 2002, Dr. Bower repaired my abdominal aortic aneurysm successfully. Unfortunately, early the next morning, I experienced a massive coronary heart attack. Evidently, a piece of plaque may have obstructed the coronary artery at that time.

I was a bit drowsy but awake when Dr. Holmes performed angioplasty by opening the blocked coronary artery without a moment's hesitation. Immediately, they reduced my blood pressure and lowered my heart rate to 80 beats per minute. Evidently, the walls of the aorta had been subjected to years and years of atherosclerosis. Even during this procedure I had no inordinate fear of death. The doctor inserted a thin tube called a catheter with a balloon at its tip through a small incision in the skin into the femoral artery in the thigh. The catheter was subsequently threaded through the connecting arteries and the aorta to my blocked artery.

The balloon was inflated and compressed the blockage and thereby opened up the artery. Then a tube made of wire mesh (a stent) was placed over the deflated balloon at the catheter's tip and was inserted with the catheter. Once the balloon was fully inflated, the stent was opened up. Accordingly, the balloon-tipped catheter was removed, and the stent was kept in place to keep the artery open.

Once the stent was inserted, I was given a drug to reduce the risk that a blood clot might block the artery again. Anyway, I was at the right place at the right time and felt most grateful since my life was saved on January 22, 2002.

After I left Mayo Clinic, I was mighty grateful to be alive. Gradually, I got back on track by getting my medication and diet in order and I started walking and jogging again. After two months of recuperation, I returned to my job as Director of the Learning Center at St. John's Northwestern Military Academy in Delafield, Wisconsin.

Unfortunately, I had my second heart attack on April 11, 2003, and recovered at Waukesha Memorial Hospital when Dr. Burns inserted a stent into the muscle of the heart so the blood flow to the arteries increased. I realized that there was more damage to the heart muscle, since the left circumflex artery had been 95% blocked.

After my first heart attack my ejection fraction (another term for cardiac efficiency) was at 40, and after my second attack, the EF is currently at 25. For some reason or other, I am not bothered by this solitary score. Although I have CHF, congestive heart failure, I don't feel congested, my heart is beating steadily, and I don't perceive any sense of failure. After my stress test, I didn't feel exhausted, and I put forth my best effort on the treadmill without overdoing it.

I decided to retire from the Military Academy in June, 2003, to avoid the pressures of teaching, and to find time to write short stories to entertain the readers.

MY OWN NEAR-DEATH EXPERIENCE

They roll me down the corridor on the gurney. The Episcopal priest blesses me. I say to her for fun, "I hope it works!" After the anesthesiologist comes by to tend to me, in one fell swoop, I leave earth and cross the threshold to Heaven. By the way, Heaven is open for verification. For sure, I know the jealous ones will say, "If Hillier gets to Heaven, then there's hope for everyone." They may even add, "How did that twillick, epithet for a fool, that Protestant, ever get past Saint Peter at the Golden Gate?"

Ha! Ha! I get used to it and so will they. "In God's name, I can't fathom this guy Hillier. He's making a travesty about his being in Heaven. You talk about such a sleeveen being saved with his unpardonable transgressions that extend far beyond those of anyone else on earth?"

I know all about the Newfie jokes and the Jarge jokes too! Jarge goes up to take his driving test. The examiner comes out and sits in the car beside him. The examiner asks, "Do you have any questions?"

"Yes! Yes! Do ye suppose it's all right if I drives around in me long rubbers?" asks Jarge.

The examiner replies, "Let's try it with the car first."

Finally, Jarge gets his license, goes to Toronto, and buys a Dodge Dart with cash on hand. The salesman tells Jarge, "You're going to love this car, but as you leave, I must remind you about one thing."

"What's that, sir?"

"This car has no reverse!"

"Don't worry about it! I won't be coming back anyway!"

The third and final joke is: Jarge is preaching in St. John's and his sermon is based on faith, hope, and charity. He does his level best to get his message across to his congregation by tying in his sermon with the Scriptures and God's holy word. After the sermon is over, an elderly parishioner comes by and says, "Young man, you had a mighty nice sermon there, but in spite of all you said, I still believe in God."

Really, though, we don't mind those jokes. It's endemic in our nature to turn the other cheek as an onward Christian soldier marching as to war.

I suppose I'm right. There's no sense grumbling about it for there are a lot of Jarge Jokes about all the Georges in Christendom.

I only need to worry about what Newfoundlanders think of me in the long run. There may still be many Torontonians, God's frozen people, who like to poke fun with their classic jokes to put the Newfies down. Newfoundlanders, though, find their subtle ways of learning to rise above the level of the upalong mediocrity.

Indeed, I feel the ecstasy of entering Heaven that is so gloriously breathtaking at the time. I see the constant angels flying to and fro like they don't know where to go, flitting about everywhere and having a ball. In the bright light, I envision their blue eyes literally dancing with laughter.

I look out into the landscape and see a little angel flying by with her condescending smile. She used to live on our street. Innocent, fresh as a daisy, just bursting in bloom and then, poof, she dies suddenly and is lost to her parents, brothers, sisters, relatives, and friends.

It's incomprehensible to think of it that way, but how can you explain life and death any other way? The parents have lost a vital part of their lives with such a tragic loss. They know she was beautiful and is now at peace. Yet, they continue to see her eyes haunting them at night and they cannot, holy or otherwise, hold back the flood of tears. Among all life's doubts and presentiments, there are always some things about life we can never understand.

Somehow they appear sensuous in their diaphanous garments and fly by to tease me with their natural flow of energy and seductive impulses; the sudden breezes they make help to cool me down a bit with their supple flashy wings.

In the evening, you can see what looks like a bank of many-tinted poplar trees in a meadow, and out beyond a range of a low cover of clouds. Heaven is purple in the evening light. What's more, it's thrilling to recognize the solemn stillness of evening by giving such a feeling of beauty and love to the entire landscape.

It's warm in Heaven which is good to know because it can't be too hot: try Hell or Dante's Inferno, if you must know. Here I have plenty of time to think and doze and dream on silken pillows of clouds, yes, to dream and sleep in the star-like besprinkled Heaven.

I see hosts of images while instinct brings me where I wish to be and, suddenly, from out of nowhere, I come face to face with my mother. Of course, we hug each other, her spirit and mine rolled in one, and my brain reels from the awakening. I am conscious of her sense and sight and then she speaks, "My son, what kept you?"

I am thinking of wise and pure and beautiful things to say and shudder for a few moments and tell her most earnestly, "Mom! I want you to know I'm only here for a visit!"

"How is that possible? Son, when you're alive, you're alive; when you're dead, you're dead. There are no two ways about it. My God, you just can't say you're here on a visit. In the meantime, welcome aboard!"

"I don't have any answers to your questions and that worries me no end. My, God, perhaps I'm dead after all."

"Up here you're in good hands. You have to face it: if you're not dead, then what are you doing here?"

"So I may have already died on the operating table?"

"Pretty likely. When you're under the knife, you have two choices: live or die. In fact, you don't have any choice in the matter. Sometimes, they say, Satan has a hand in it. He is often known to opine, 'Stand not upon the order of your going, but go at once!' One thing about life, you can't beat the rap forever."

"Gee! I don't know what to do with myself."

"Don't worry about it. 'Tis already done. You don't have to make any excuses for yourself."

"I'm sorry! I believe I made a fool of myself. Dr. Bower, the night before my operation, told me I had nothing to worry about. He was mostly concerned in looking at the x-rays."

"Do you know you're supposed to have two adrenal glands?"

"Yes! I know that."

"You know what?"

"What?"

"You have four adrenal glands."

"In that case, doctor, you can get rid of the other two."

"No! No! That's to your advantage. I will keep them all intact."

"Thank you, doctor!"

"You know, Mom, I shouldn't have to worry. I've gone beyond the Biblical three score and ten. If I died on the operating table, so be it. I refuse to be a sooky (whiner). All I have to do is to get caught up in the scheme of things in Heaven."

"I assure you, there are no schemes here! That's for sure. Just kiss earth goodbye and say hello to Heaven. You should feel darned lucky to be here."

So, finally, I get it. As a believer, I am part of the resurrected life. I, like others, have been begotten again by the resurrection of Jesus Christ from the dead. I comply and rise from the dead. Yet I reckon myself to be alive unto God in Christ Jesus. Therefore, I settle in and follow the path of righteousness in God who lives in me.

"You see, Mom, I'm in the midst of having

an operation on my aorta at the Mayo Clinic in Rochester, Minnesota, and I'm waiting for the operation to end before I return. Don't worry. I have a good chance of survival."

"Well, that's nice to know. It's soothing to hear some good news for a change."

I have to tell her as much as I can without bothering her a lot. "It's been a long, long time, Mom; how are you getting on?"

She tells me about the smooth landscapes where angels are singing and chanting about the loveliest things happening in Heaven. I remember, though, when we were young, she came out of the pantry with a little pad and I happened to read it when it was left on the kitchen table, "Into each life some rain must fall." The other point she used to espouse was this advice to her family, "You make your own Heaven and Hell on Earth." I still believe in the wisdom of her philosophy. On earth, things never seem to end up the way she would like them to be, but up here she reaches the greatest heights of her ecstasy.

Also, I remember, Jason Jones, who lives in the city. He was, undoubtedly, a devout Roman Catholic and his parents expressed high hopes for his future. "Jason," his mother used to say, "I am certain as stars in the heavens, I will live to see you a bishop yet. Mark my words."

It was pretty much settled and Jason received

distinctions at his seminary. In the beginning, he was showing good signs of religious zeal, but after two years, he began to feel doubts about himself. He was more and more convinced that he could not accept the doctrines for which he had been educated. Finally, he couldn't stand it anymore and told his parents that he must give up taking the Holy Orders.

There was never a problem with his church or theological studies, but, after much agonizing, he knew he was hopelessly in love and realized, try as he did, the stark reality that he could never become celibate. Indeed, he was in torment for some time and told me about the feeling of being suspended in the depths of darkness, in doubt and despair.

Nevertheless, his parents were most loving and most understanding of his situation. At the time, Jason told me, "George, as much as I loved the idea of becoming a priest, it's nice to know what you're not fitted for in life."

Having been his friend, I can recognize the intrinsic depths of his character: the embodiment of truth, charity, and respect for his loyalty to the cloth.

"Why did you bring Jason Jones up?"

"Since you remember him, I thought I'd speak about him to fill you in on what's going on down below these days. I thought you'd be interested?"

"O! I am. Is Jason alive or dead?"

"He's very much alive and he's enjoying his retirement."

My mother's overwhelming passion intrigues me. I study her eyes as soon as she tells me, "The good thing about Heaven is that we don't have to shed tears anymore. God gives us free rein on our lives for that matter. And we earn His perfect love as well as perfect justice through that love. He's not really concerned about us, but He is more worried as to what's happening on earth. Remember the expression, 'Going to Hell in a hand basket'? Well, that's exactly what's happening down below."

"You're absolutely right. It goes back to the Bible—the money-changers for one thing. I fully remember my great-grandmother, Jessie Caroline Wilcox Cassidy, teaching me about the money-changers in Saint Matthew.

"And Jesus went into the temple of God, and cast out all them that sold and bought in the temple, and overthrew the tables of the money-changers, and the seats of them that sold doves.

And He said unto them, 'It is written, My house shall be called the house of prayer; but ye have made it a den of thieves.' " (Matthew: 21: 12-13)

"How do you like Heaven so far, son?"

"I love it here if you must know. Certainly,

it gives me a little time to dance on rainbow-coloured clouds. I sure know 'tis great to be here to know God is the one who sticks to His promise in a secretive way. I was just reading the other day in the ninth chapter of Second Chronicles. It says the Queen of Sheba, ruler of Ethiopia, observes all that God had done for Solomon and said, 'Blessed be the Lord thy God, which delighted in thee to set thee on His throne, to be king for the Lord thy God: because thy God loved Israel, to establish them forever, therefore made thee king over them, to do judgment and justice.' "

Here we see the Queen of Sheba praising God because He was the answer to Solomon's prayer. Moreover, she believed that God's promise was made since she speaks of His establishing Israel forever. In turn, God was so pleased to hear the Queen of Sheba's compliments and never forgot them.

"You know, George, a friend of mine, Martha Thomas, sings songs and reads poetry once in awhile to my intrinsic delight. Would you like to hear one of her songs she wrote the other night?"

"By all means. Go ahead. Anyway, you know I love poetry and songs."

"It is a sweet and saving thing
To feel your handclasp in the night.

A curious, swift answering
To loneliness and sudden fright.
Palm white palm, all squarely filled,
The fingers gripping tight and strong,
Until the clanging terror's killed,
That woke the heart up like a gong.
Who smells perfume in a rose?
Or sees a bird song being wrought
In one lark's feathered throat?
The reach of love, the shape of thought?
It is the warm, deep comforting
To feel your fingers gripping tight;
The touch of sweet remembering,
In lonely watches of the night."

"That's marvelous, Mom! I didn't know they wrote poetry in Heaven too."

"O, yes! That's the way it is. We sing our songs and recite our poems up here all the time. I want you to know, we keep up with everything. We're not in the Dark Ages like down below, you know."

"Do you do plays too?"

"Once in a blue moon."

"That's good to know. I will remember that in the future. In other words, when I get to Heaven full-time, that is, if there's some chance I may be the chosen one, I will keep writing poetry as long as I can."

"Of course! By all means. Life is proverbial,

anyway. We can even break into a jubilant song in a moment's notice. Listen as we invoke Heaven to lead the strain, 'Sing, O Heaven, and be joyful for it's our choice—to break forth into singing to the mountains for the Lord comforts us and we rejoice.' "

"Mom, I see things more clearly since you are more comforted by the Lord in your dwelling place. Now, Mom, I am running out of time, and I must get back before Dr. Bower finishes stitching up my aorta. However, that reminds me, I must see Dad before I go. But before I do, do you mind if I ask you a question?"

"Certainly not! Shoot!"

"What is the essential difference between Heaven up here and the Earth down below?"

"As God is my judge, I love it here. We have our own spirit of living far better than on earth. Above all, we are grateful and content and say our hallelujahs to the Lord God Omnipotent."

"I dare say, Mom, there is something else you would like to tell me. I have a hunch there's something else you'd like to say. What's the matter, Mom? Tell me: are you vexed? What ails you?"

In the spectral loveliness of the day, my mother appears calm, but she comes closer to me and whispers: "Keep this under your hat. Once in awhile, I get tongue-tied and I don't know what to say, but something or other comes to mind. Don't get me wrong; life up here is perfect felicity. I must admit I do get a sudden touch of nostalgia that expresses my own heart's desire: 'To tell the truth, son, I miss home most of all.' "

"Mom, before I go, I sure would love to talk with Dad. Do you know where he might be?"

"Let me tell you, you don't have to worry about your father. He's just over there on Cloud Nine cavorting with the angels."

I kiss my mother and say goodbye. Then I float along and remember my father when he was on earth, seeing him whistling away and working hard at everything he did so well. But that was many years ago. Suddenly, I see him from a distance and when we meet, he says,

"My son, my son, what have you done? You're a sight for sore eyes!" We hug each other and talk about the early years, especially our trouting times together on Salmonier Line.

"How are things going with you, Dad?"

"Grand, my son! The finest kind! Things couldn't be better up here on the Higher Levels. I feel some lucky for I was never sure of Heaven, but I am now, thank God."

"Son, I must ask you, how goes the battle with you? I'm rightly concerned."

"I'm having an operation on my aorta.

So I ended up here after my body was sedated."

"Glory be! Well now, if that doesn't take the cake. Listen! Your grandfather, the Salvationist, George Hillier, died of an aneurysm at the age of 36. The Lord save us. I guess it's all relative, though. But I'm still concerned for your health. Keep me posted, will you?"

"Of course! Today this sort of operation is quite successful. Although I'm 73, my surgeon tells me I'll be all right. They work wonders today in the medical world. Anyway, if I don't make it, I'll let you know."

"What are you talking about, son?"

"Sorry, Dad, that's my senior moment for today. Janemarie tells me I'm allowed one senior moment a day and that was it. I mean if I should die, I dare say, I might have a chance of getting to Heaven, legitimately, if that's possible at all. Besides, I'll cross that bridge when I come to it. Anyway, I got enough to worry about now. Do you really like it here, Dad, or are you just putting me on?"

"I'm up in Heaven now where I belong. Guaranteed! In fact, son, there is no place I'd rather be than here. For the benefit of the ignorant ones on earth, tell them when you return that there's plenty of camaraderie here in Heaven. Every day is a day of prayer and thanksgiving. That's the way it is. I'm content and downright pleased."

"Why do you have to pray if you're already in Heaven?"

"Good question. We don't pray for ourselves. We've already arrived. Instead, we pray for those poor angishores, poverty stricken creatures, down below. To be sure, they have their own crosses to bear."

"I never met your father, Dad, can you tell me about him?"

"He was a millwright at the site where Bennett Avenue is today. He was a sergeant-major in the Salvation Army and, believe you me, he was mighty strict."

"Would you believe it, Dad, I have a snap of your family when you lived on Alexander Street years ago?"

"You do? I can't believe you still have it after all those years."

"I'm the collector, remember? In the Hillier line-up in front of your house were: Jack, Blanche, June, Elsie, and yourself. Do you know what's so funny about the picture, Dad?"

"No! What?"

"You're all standing rigidly at attention."

"That's right. There's no doubt about it. For sure, your grandfather was a firm disciplinarian and a deeply religious man."

"Dad, I still have a poem, the one he kept when he sang in memory of the founder of the Salvation Army. The title is "When General

William Booth Enters Heaven." It was written by Vachel Lindsay. This stanza is the last of seven in all:

"And when Booth halted by the curb for
  prayer
He saw his Master through the flag-filled air.
Christ came gently with a robe and crown
For Booth the soldier while the throng knelt
  down.
He saw King Jesus. They were face to face,
And he knelt a-weeping in that holy place.
Are you washed in the blood of the Lamb?"

"Dad, I'll be off soon, but I have just one question for you: what advantage does Heaven have over Earth below?"

"My God, son! That's easy! Up here you don't have to pay the light bill!"

A SONNET ON SURVIVING TWO HEART ATTACKS

God save me from the measured blow of
    death
And hear me as I make one plea for grace
For time will stop when I run out of breath
Yet hide me from the wounds that leave their
    trace.
O! Strengthen me to learn to bear my cross
For in such time of pain and loneliness
I surely look for hope to gain from loss
That I may see above the emptiness.
I am so tired, so changeable, and frail:
Time knows what needs there are for love
    and praise
When life is hard at times for those who fail
Then wish the heart for comfort on those
    days.
So I may live to dull the edge of pain
And find such pleasure in my life again.

CRY FOR HELP!

I must tell you that I received a letter and a gift on December 23, 2004, from John Warren who lives in Massachusetts. I was somewhat surprised and yet pleased to hear from him. This same letter gives John's accounting of what happened to him at Sebago Lake in Naples, Maine, in August 2004:

"It was Monday, the second week of August, 2004. My son, Craig Warren, had left over the weekend with his fourteen year old daughter, and taken her home to Massachusetts. My daughter, Melanie, had gone home to Massachusetts, that weekend, because her three daughters, Courtney, Kendall, and Carly, had been entered in a swim meet. My granddaughter, Courtney, won the competition for her age category. They arrived at Sebago Lake State Park that Sunday evening. My son, Craig, left his younger daughter, Kerri, with us when he returned home on that weekend.

"My wife, Fran, was a lifeguard and waterfront director at summer camps when she was in high school and college. On that Monday, Sebago Lake was turbulent and the kids had gone out in kayaks in the morning and found the waters of the lake were rough. Fran let her daughter, Melanie, know that the lake was too dangerous for her and her children to paddle those waters. Melanie, however, didn't realize how dangerous it was.

"Melanie's middle daughter, Kendall, was fearful of going into the lake. In the meantime, Melanie's oldest daughter, Courtney, spoke to my wife about how rough the waters were in the morning. Fran felt that the kayakers should take bungee cords and connect the kayaks so they'd be together in case the wind got worse. Courtney followed my wife's suggestions.

"Here I was sitting on my chair near the lake when Melanie asked me if I would like to go out in a two-seater. At that time, Fran was in the shade quite a ways from the action along with Kendall, who decided to stay on shore. For sure I wasn't interested in going out on the lake at all. Melanie looked out over the lake near your house and Courtney (Melanie's daughter) and Carly (Melanie's youngest daughter) had each taken out a single kayak. My son's daughter, Kerri, also was in a single kayak. When the kayaks were on their way, Melanie and the kids had a hard time maneuvering in the water. Melanie observed that Courtney had fallen out of her kayak.

"I got alarmed and Melanie and I got in a two-seater kayak and got over near your side of the lake in a hurry. I had never been in a kayak before. Melanie got in the stern while I got in the bow. Melanie also gave me instructions on how to operate the kayak. We found out later that Courtney was in the water because the wind had pushed the three kayaks towards the shore. She did hitch the kayaks together. Now Melanie and I were desperately trying to avoid bumping into the other kayaks. I was trying to stabilize the kayak by pushing down on the paddle. Just at that moment the kayak tipped over and I ended up in the water and was still holding on to the paddle.

"Unfortunately, I never wore a life jacket. I should have listened when Melanie told me to put a life jacket on. I didn't do it because I was anxious to get to the girls to help them in their time of need. Once in the water, I started to swim to the shore with my left hand while my right hand was holding on to the paddle. Every time I moved a little further, the wind kept pushing me back to the west of me. The paddle was also dragging me. I was swallowing water and I felt my strength was weakening. I was worried for I was feeling pains in my chest. I didn't feel I had enough strength to continue. My chest was so tight; it was then I called out for help. Melanie, though, thought that I was safe, figuring I had a life jacket on, and just told me to hang on to the paddle.

"When I called for help, she never realized how much trouble I was in. I was desperate and called out for help many times. The last time I called out, I said, 'Jesus, save me! Have mercy on me, a sinner!' That is exactly when my savior, George Hillier, came on the scene."

My account on saving John Warren's life:

I usually take a nap after lunchtime for about 40 minutes or so and slept in the back bedroom where it is a quiet escape from the noise on the beach. As I began to wake up, I thought I heard a sound, not the mere noise and shouts of children swimming out there with motor boats and sail boats on Sebago Lake. Amid all the activity going on, I was especially aware of a sound that seemed urgent, saying, "Jesus, save me!" For sure it was a real voice calling out for immediate help. I had my clothes on along with my sneakers and got up off my bed and ran through the house for I couldn't restrain myself any longer. My lifeguard training from years ago suddenly kicked into high gear. My wife, Janemarie, was in the kitchen and asked me, "Where are you going?" I answered her without stopping, "To the point! Someone needs help out there!" When I was on my deck, I could see a figure was calling out for help so I ran as fast as my legs could carry me. If the man had drowned before I got to him, then I would have blamed myself for not getting to him sooner. I felt that I should have taken a life jacket with me; yet I didn't, for time was of the essence in such a case as this. If I had to swim from my area of the beach to where the person was in the lake, then for certain, I would have been too tired to rescue him. Besides, I saved a lot of valuable time. I ran beyond my neighbors' log cabin, owned by the Cole family. I sped over the rocks along the shore and then took a trail that led me to Cuneo's Point.

I noticed that the wind had come up and there was a man who had fallen out of his kayak. He was a heavy-set man who was bobbing up and down and crying out for help. He was in over his head and was dragging a paddle behind him. No power on earth could have taken my eyes away from his face at that moment. From my viewpoint, his eyes told me he was desperate and, no doubt, entirely lost in his own imaginings. Evidently, he had taken in a lot of water and was hawking and coughing and trying to catch his breath in his plight. When I reached the point, I shouted out to him, "Sir! Put both hands on your paddle and kick your feet!" There was a young woman on shore and some children near her. Also, there were kayaks that were beached. I dove in the lake and swam towards the man who was less than 100 yards away from me. He looked exhausted and perhaps in some state of shock.

When I got close to him, I told him to keep holding on to the paddle with both hands and keep kicking his feet. I certainly didn't want him to grab hold of me because we could both have gone under together. I was treading water and kept my hands underneath his stomach area so he could breathe more easily. He was frothing at the mouth and said to me, "My God, you're my savior!" I looked at him and said, "Thanks all the same, sir. I just want to get you to the shore."

Once I got the man to shore, I took off his shirt, and then had him lie prone on the warm beach sand. I checked his mouth and spoke to him quietly, yet I don't believe he was fully conscious of what he was saying since he seemed to be still in a state of shock from his near-death experience. I could tell, though, that he seemed somewhat relieved to be safe on shore.

Shortly after I put my arm around the man, and we walked slowly together to our cottage where my wife, Janemarie, was waiting for us. I was alarmed when Janemarie spoke to the survivor, "Sir, do you realize that my husband has had two heart attacks and his life was in danger, too!" Nevertheless, she made hot chocolate for John and his daughter, along with her children!

At the time, the local papers wanted to write

about this incident, but I didn't think it was necessary. Anyway, it's always a comforting thought in times of trouble when life triumphs over death.

When Christmas 2004 arrived, Janemarie and I received a card from the John Warren family. It was heartwarming to receive John's blessings:

"Dear George and Janemarie,

I hope you are well up in Wisconsin. I will always be most grateful to you for having saved my life. God Bless you now and always.

Love,

John and Frances Warren"

Furthermore, we have remained close friends ever since.

In retrospect, I never really believed I was a hero except to say we are our brother's keeper.

NEW YEAR

In this troubled world of humanity
Let our faith bloom and never fade away
By seeking inner calm and sanity
With gifts of peace wrapped up in love today.
Casting aside past sorrows, grief and pain,
But enriched in hope and patient in prayer,
We begin a new year over again
In finding courage is still present here.
Let us take precious moments of each hour
And turn them into an eternity
By growing in God's image and power
To live with honor, grace, and ecstasy.
Let us feel the touch of a loving hand
Or just a smile to help us understand.

COMMENTARIES ON
UNIQUELY HUMAN

"George Hillier writes with wit, insight and optimism about the joys of being human gleaned from a rich lifetime of serving others. His generous spirit comes through in a light-hearted way, pairing philosophical prose with peppery puns. You'll savor his stories, pause to reflect, and smile. Enjoy!"

> *Audrey Kurth Cronin, Professor at the U.S. National War College. Senior Research Associate in the Changing Character of War Program, at Oxford University*

"George Hillier is my hero for his life of success from adversity. He is a brilliant man who loves and appreciates the colorful culture of Newfoundland, the land of our ancestors. His tales of that wonderful island are a great joy to me. I am proud to call him both my cousin and my friend."

> *Captain Alfred J. Dillon, USN, Ret.*

"This book by George Wilcox Hillier is the culmination of a long-standing interest in expressing himself through the written word. His stories, many of which are based on his experience of growing up in St. John's, Newfoundland, in the 1930's and 1940's, have the ability to capture one's imagination, to evoke a mood, to stir one's emotions, and to inform one's mind. George Hillier has the ability not only to amuse and to entertain, but also to uplift and to inspire. Moreover, his powers of description are such that at times one feels drawn into the scenes he so vividly describes."

Dr. Morley Hodder, D.Th., D.D.,
Professor Emeritus of Religious
Studies, (Ret.), Memorial University
of Newfoundland, St. John's,
Newfoundland, Canada

"George Hillier is a splendid scholar and teacher throughout his life. He was an athlete as a schoolboy and in his college years. When he works with his cadets, he doesn't just demand work from them in his learning center, but nurtures and inspires them to reach for the best level of productivity in their academics. George continues to teach and is a distinct inspiration to all the many lives he has touched in his lifetime."

Lyman McLallen, Assistant Professor
of Foreign Studies, Hankuk
University, Seoul, South Korea

"George Hillier's uplifting writings mingle prose and poetry. Despite his health challenges, the author has a positive outlook on life. I enjoyed the gentle humor in his work that shares his thoughts and experiences. Reading his book will put a smile on your face."

Charlotte Robinson, retired teacher

"George Hillier is a prolific writer. His grasp of all things human should be a primer of life to all of us. This man's gentle spirit embraces all the good things virtuous people seek."

Jack H. Albert, Jr., President,
St. John's Northwestern Military
Academy, Delafield, Wisconsin

"George Hillier is a talented writer and an inspirational friend. His book captures the best things about life and provides encouragement for the soul."

John Thornburg, M.S., Dean of
Students, St. John's Northwestern
Military Academy, Delafield,
Wisconsin

"George Hillier is gregarious, soft-spoken, artistic, religious, and his writing is inspirational to read. I believe you will enjoy his company when you read his book."

Joseph R. Storrs, Ph.D., Research &
Development Coordinator

"George, you are one of the most kind hearted individuals I have crossed paths with. Your wisdom and love for life are beyond words. I am honored to say you started as a teacher to me and are now a friend forever. The title of your book says it all."

Aaron Jeremias, former student,
St. John's Northwestern Military
Academy, Delafield, Wisconsin

Center Point Large Print
600 Brooks Road / PO Box 1
Thorndike, ME 04986-0001 USA

(207) 568-3717

US & Canada:
1 800 929-9108
www.centerpointlargeprint.com